Margaret Connelly

Talk of the Parish

GOD BLESS FR O'SHEA

Published by
Liverpool Authors
54 Brows Lane
Formby
L37 4ED

Printed by
Ribcar (Liverpool) Ltd
56 Lower Breck Road
Tuebrook, Liverpool
L6 4BZ

Contents

	Acknowledgement	1
Chapter 1	In the Beginning	4
Chapter 2	Back to Your Roots	12
Chapter 3	Do You Remember?	17
Chapter 4	Special Moments Grand Times ...	27
Chapter 5	The Evacuees	36
Chapter 6	Queen of the Angels ...	49
Chapter 7	Golden Memories	58
Chapter 8	Her Name Was Mary	72
Chapter 9	The GIs	81
Chapter 10	The Blessed Healing Petals	89
Chapter 11	Traditions	99
Chapter 12	Memories Last Longer ...	111
Chapter 13	The Late Mrs Catherhan	115
Chapter 14	Those Were The Days	124
Chapter 15	Wedding Cake	137

ACKNOWLEDGEMENTS

M y second book Talk of the Parish has been a trifle easier to pen than my first novel My Parish Holy Cross. My heart was truly broken at the time when our beautiful church finally closed, those once welcoming doors now closed for ever.

My thanks to my loving family who continue to give me the strength to overcome the whingeing and soldier on. To my precious granddaughter Katie Donnelly who is a whiz on the computer without her expertise, I would have truly been floundering. Special thanks as usual must go to my extra special friend Rose Roach who continually supplied me with endless cups of coffee to stimulate the tired mind, along with her special homemade scrumptious culinary delights. Thanks girl! To my good friend Ron Formby whose help and use of the fabulous community paper 'The Scottie Press'. Ron truly beats the drum for many of us who are ever struggling to finance our work, but with a little help from friends we do eventually go on to publish the end product.

As usual the assistance of my old friends and neighbours of my wonderful supportive parish of Holy Cross, especially Tommy (Golly) Gallagher for unlocking his own precious and valued chest of memorable photographs. Which indeed are priceless! I know how privileged I was for Tommy to give me possession and most importantly of all permission, to use for this book, thanks lad! A special thank you to my forever [helpful] friends Irene Hanratty, Wally Hesdon for his generous help, in promoting my book at the Shrine of the Blessed Sacrament Piety shop. Bligh's newsagents, Joan and Tony McGann of the Eldonians. A big thanks to my English tutor Margaret Davey, who helped refresh my memory on the correct use of adjectives and verbs. God Bless you all for your on going encouragement and solid support.

Arrival of the Irish Immigrants in the early 1800s including my grandparents along with thousands of others who made their life and home in the inner city to create vibrant communities including our own 'little Ireland' in the parish of Holy Cross.

I am dedicating this latest book to my Irish Grandparents Edward and Winifred Gildea who along with thousands more Irish Immigrants chose to settle and make their home in our fabulous City of Liverpool. (The rest is indeed history).

Reliving a wonderful childhood inspired by my caring parents, our splendid clergy. Our teachers from Infants [Miss Craven] to the juniors [Mr Smith], senior class [Miss Haynes] who invariably helped shape our lives, always striving for the best possible opportunities in order to prepare us to compete for a decent career. I sincerely thank them all for they did an exceptional job in educating the cheeky but lovable urchins of Holy Cross. We were extremely fortunate in having such a

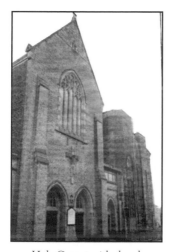

Holy Cross parish church
Standish Street.

The Pieta which was removed from Holy Cross church; It stands in Standish Street where ironically the first Holy Cross church was established.

team of dedicated teaching staff advising us both spiritually and bodily. I have yet to find the appropriate words in describing the binds that so strongly bond the people of Holy Cross, right up to this present day.

I can honestly say hand on heart I have never once ceased in thinking that my parish Holy Cross, will always and ever mean home to me. When I did eventually leave the parish to begin married life we still continued to attend Sunday Mass at Holy Cross eventually to be joined by our two off-spring Tommy and Lisa. Don't they say a happy home is always were the heart chooses to remain. Amen!

CHAPTER ONE

IN THE BEGINNING

It was in the year 1846 when the exodus of Irish immigrants begun. The streets of Liverpool were swarming with starving ragged clad Irish people. These poor unfortunates did not exactly want to be in Liverpool, the true fact of their situation was the failure of their potato crops. They were cruelly driven from their abodes with little more than what they were standing up in at the time. Landing at Liverpool hoping to find any type of employment and seek a roof over their heads. Many had high hopes of travelling to America, the majority of the immigrants settled in the south end of the city although some did settle north too. The poor destitute souls slept in any available space they could find, huddled together in condemned properties without any form of heat during the coldest months of the winter.

The sad fact is the Vauxhall area was having the worst records of premature deaths in the community, especially the children. Sixty-five out of a hundred children were dying before reaching the tender age of eight. The good people of Liverpool responded, every denomination pitched in to alleviate the suffering. Fever sheds were quickly set up in the surrounding areas of the inner city. A hospital ship was hastily prepared which was berthed on the river Mersey. Indeed there was an enormous job to be tackled but by who? At the time there were certainly no willing takers. The already established churches of St Anthony and St Mary's were desperately struggling to cope; such was the influx of Irish Catholics into Liverpool. It took almost four years before any action was taken to alleviate the problem. The parish priest at Saint Anthony's arranged for holy mass to be celebrated in a ramshackle room directly above a cowshed in Standish Street.

This somewhat dilapidated abode was later adapted to become a temporary church donated by a generous Irish businessman a Mr Sam Moreton.

The temporary church was opened on the 25th of March 1849. The poor but now happy people flocked to the church delighted in having their own church to worship at. Not a few yards away in Standish Street stood an ancient cross from early times erected in honour of Saint Patrick; it is no folklore, as it is clearly marked on old maps of Liverpool. Saint Patrick had stood on that very spot before continuing his journey to Ireland. How fitting that the new church should be sited so near the parish Church of Holy Cross was finally up and running.

OUR FIRST PARISH PRIEST

The priests at Saint Anthony's parish Father Newsham and Father Nugent were seriously struggling with the overload of pastoral work. The Bishop of Liverpool at the time was Bishop Brown; he negotiated with an Irish Order, the Oblates of Mary Immaculate, eventually handing over the mission church to their capable care. On the 18th of January 1850 Father Noble arrived to become the first parish priest of Holy Cross church. Eventually another three missionary priests arrived to assist Father Noble. Father Noble set about transforming the parish. This resilient priest immediately took the parishioners straight into his overzealous heart, promising them with their continued help, he and his fellow priests would build schools, but most of all a close knit and caring community. For the next couple of years Father Noble and his hardworking assistants worked unstintingly to achieve what he had promised. This wonderful industrious priest had in no time at all, truly transformed the entire parish, he had given hope to the poor people, instilling his enthusiasm through to them. A terrifically strong bond was quickly moulded at the onset of the arrival of the Missionary Fathers the Oblates of Mary Immaculate. That bond would continue to grow even stronger over the decades. Holy Cross parish grew in strength becoming the Oblates first missionary church in England.

THE VISIT OF BISHOP EUGENE DE MAZENOD

Eugene De Mazenod was a Frenchman who later became Bishop of Marseilles, he founded the Oblate Order. The respected name of the Oblate order soon spread through-out Europe. It seemed the Oblate's were spreading their good works through-out towns where religion was sadly non-existent, because of the chronic shortage of priests. In June 1850 our venerable founder travelled to Liverpool to witness for himself the newly established parish of Holy Cross. What a welcome he received, thousands of poor Irish parishioners lined the streets. Bishop Eugene celebrated Benediction in the evening. He was later stated to have said he was indeed truly humbled and overwhelmed by the sheer out-pouring of their faith and reverence for him.

The Bishop was visibly moved, in fact to tears as each in turn fell to their knees, kissing the hem of his robes, seizing his hand to kiss and hold it to their foreheads. How the people appreciated the Bishops gesture in taking time out to visit his poor flock that truly were mere peasants. The Bishop was accompanied by thousands of fervent parishioners, cheering enthusiastically every step he took until arriving at the presbytery. Blessing the crowds once again, thanking them over and over again in his native tongue. Once again the Bishop was visibly moved, this time when witnessing working men kneeling with so much reverence holding their caps in their hands.

Demonstrations of total and utter respect on show from tough hardworking men really humbled this charismatic man. Walking amongst the men sharing his blessings placing his hands on their shoulders, here was the man, the 'Boss' of their beloved clergy, extending his welcomed blessings to them. The visit from the 'Boss' was a phenomenal success, so much so after his visit the four priests were working over-time hearing confessions. Hundreds of lapsed Catholics returned to their faith as a result of Bishop Mazenods visit. It certainly was the talk of the parish for months on end. Every one was in total agreement this exceptional man was truly *'a walking saint'*, the people of Holy Cross recognized this the moment they set eyes on him, and they were to be proved right many years later.

FATHER NOBLE'S ACHIEVEMENTS

In Holy Cross folklore Father Noble was a dynamic personality bent  on making life easier for his desperate poor and disadvantaged parishioners. Father Noble's door was always ajar ready to help and advise them and not always on religious issues. My Dad loved to talk about Father Noble's escapades especially when his cousin Eddie Callaghan visited our house for his tea. They reminisced together talking about him as if he was a hero or a legend of the movie world. Constantly recalling Father Noble's many triumphs. None sweeter, when the result was against the establishment. Not afraid of a good scrap, he seldom walked away a loser either chuckled my Dad. There were many hard disputes in those dark days of Religious divide, blood flowed shockingly, staining the streets of Liverpool, Especially Irish Catholics blood they were easy targets and were treated very shabbily indeed. Thankfully we have come a long way since. My uncle Eddie so admired Father Noble he'd fondly reminisce about the way he'd cleverly outwit the smartest politician or lawyer, they wouldn't live with Father Noble my uncle Eddie bragged proudly. All these numerous tales kept alive lovingly in order to be handed down from one generation to the other. Father Noble's hands on approach united the people of Holy Cross they really loved the bones of this honest and workaholic priest. Respect, strong bonds of affection are characteristic of the Holy Cross people, which have been strongly demonstrated throughout the 152 years to which I personally and proudly can vouch for. Up until the day the church doors finally closed ending 152 years of glorious and illustrious occasions, a sad day indeed.

Father Noble was a highly intelligent and learned man in his own right, he successfully lead an enquiry against the local police force, for using brute and unnecessary force against his parishioners. He lamented that the police officers should be impartial protectors and certainly not the aggressors as they had so viciously and brutally attacked Roman Catholics so readily. Winning the case against the police was indeed a momentous result for the whole of the Catholic communities, how true the saying, the fountain pen being mightier than the sword, certainly came to fruition the people of the city, highly impressed once again, being guided by this invincible man (he was to his parishioners). An Irish mogul was so influenced by the firm stance took by the strong willed priest, he generously handed him a substantial amount of money to boost the school funds. Requesting that he inform him when he starts his next project the building of the new church. January the 16th 1854 saw the grand and proud opening of Holy Cross School. After celebrating mass the children walked in procession to their brand new school, headed by the clergy. Following on behind was hundreds of grateful parishioners so proud for their children who now had the opportunity to an education, something they never had, it was indeed a momentous day for the parishioners. Each classroom in turn was blessed, the nuns standing by to welcome the urchins of Holy Cross into their new classrooms. Father Noble eventually introduced evening classes which were a tremendous success. In order to help educate the working men and women of the parish as much as three quarters of them were in ignorance of the three 'R's, that situation was soon to change.

It was not only the Holy Cross people who were in debt to Father Noble the Catholics of Liverpool too owing so much to this forthright clergyman. In an extraordinary short space of time, he helped transform the lives of so many eager people desperately wanting to educate themselves; they came in their droves to attend the adult evening classes held at Holy Cross School. Father Noble's venture was pronounced as a pioneering gamble that had paid off handsomely. He was the special one who would represent them, the ordinary people, he had the courage to challenge and out fox the cleverest establishment, in those dark days of religious conflict. Thankfully we have come a long way since those barbaric times when blood was shed time and again on to the streets of our city. After six long years of sheer hard graft and so many splendid achievements, the dreaded announcement was that Father Noble was to be moved on to another deserving parish.

The untimely decision broke the hearts of not only Holy Cross parishioners but also people throughout the archdioceses. Father Noble's next appointment was to a parish in Leith, he was as saddened as his beloved flock were, he found it tremendously hard going, having to take his leave from these wonderful people who had taken him close within their grateful hearts. Such a bond of trust, respect, and sheer adulation for their leader had grown immensely in his time spent here, the feelings were totally mutual. My Dad told me on the day Father Noble set off for his new appointment. The whole of the parish turned out, men, women and children lined the streets to wave him goodbye. Singing with fervour an old fashioned and revered hymn, 'Faith of our Fathers', which we love and always associate it with our Catholic faith. Even more parishioners joined the procession marching in step behind him to the train station. It was one sad day for the people of Holy Cross; this wonderful sound man that was so instrumental in changing their sorry lives forever. When opening the door to education and gave them back their self-esteem, quite a gift indeed. He will mostly be remembered as the pioneer priest who paved the way, in putting the GOOD name of Holy Cross and their people into the Oblate manual he helped create the deserved and earned mantle, of 'the jewel in the crown'.

THE END OF AN ERA

I think it is safe to declare it was no secret the *establishment* was not the only body grateful to see the back of Father Noble, it was a dark day when the news was received that Father Noble had died tragically on the 1st of April 1867 the entire parish fell into deep mourning for their gallant hero. He was in the prime of his life 44 years of age. My Dad adamantly maintained his death was no accident, (again the folklore of the parish kicks in, guarded and, graciously handed down from one generation to another). It was a known fact that Father Noble was an exceptional swimmer and no possible way would he drown, he was a fit strong individual, as always fighting the good fight against difficult and uncooperative opposition.

The parishioners of Holy Cross were devastated by his premature death and were never totally convinced that his death was accidental as reported by the authorities. It was alleged that he might have stumbled losing his balance while walking along the jetty in the dock area, an area in which he was well accustomed to as he walked the familiar route every night. It was alleged that he became encumbered by his heavy cloak which he wore that fateful night. It was also reported that it was an exceptionally windy night, making swimming impossible even for the most experienced swimmer. The people of Holy Cross however thought otherwise, but the authority's predicted verdict was accepted as gospel, accidental death. My Dad talked often with so much affection about this incredible man who certainly became a hero to the working class people of Liverpool he fought relentlessly for the rights of all people not only our Irish ancestors of which we are truly grateful. Father Noble a genuine and true working class hero to the people of Liverpool.

The rest is history, another Church was erected after the first, which was described as a mini cathedral because of the sheer beauty of its interior. Cruelly desecrated by enemy fire in the Second World War known as the May blitz. The severe bombing almost wiped out the residents of Lace Street, it was a bitter blow, claiming the lives and cruelly wiping out a whole generation. Against crude built brick wall eight coffins, all related, lay side-by-side united in death in one small terraced house. How sad is that innocent victims of war, the parish suffered dreadfully in that awful month of the war. Again that never say die spirit and total loyalty was to be tested once again. Against all the odds funds were raised once more in order to rebuild on the original site. Holy Cross once again was celebrating in style. Dancing in the streets, true to form celebrations ongoing for a week or more, thousands descended on the parish enjoying the colourful and joyous sights, admiring the lavish decorations. Fast forward once again to the year 1999 when we gathered in our magnificent church in Standish Street to celebrate our noble heritage steeped in glorious traditions the likes of which we will never ever witness again. Here we are again together cherishing 150 years of parish life in Holy Cross, what a feat! The hierarchy of the diocese assembled to hand out bouquets acknowledging the achievements of our famous and renowned parish. To the memory of our ancestors who down through the years responded to the impossible challenges of building a solid community made up of years of resourcefulness sometimes having to buck the system (what a system). Celebrating in the Avril Robarts hall, reunited with our past teachers and clergy, as always recalling golden and magical occasions, throwing in a few Irish jigs and reels for good measure.

Two years down the line our cherished place of worship was to be taken out of divine service. How empty those accolades and bouquets read now, very bitter, none terribly sweet. September 16th 2001 we worshiped for the last time no sign or presence of the dignitaries on this occasion, only the ghosts of yesterday's glory times being re-enacted in our memories. Devastated parishioners past and present were in attendance. Silently we whispered our good-byes. Born and reared precious occasions in your life that are priceless, golden, no hang on I'd say platinum. Now there's a monstrous block of so-called luxury apartments erected on the exact spot where our adored parish church once stood. At least we have the return of our most treasured and loved Pieta statue lovingly cared for standing in a garden of community memories. The completion of the history of our parish of Holy Cross privileged in the early years, in having had the company of two glorious Saints walk our once vibrant streets. Saint Patrick Patron Saint of Ireland, our very own Saint Eugene De Mazenod, our founder and forever friend of the community who helped re-write the illustrious history of Holy Cross.

The day of the opening of Holy Cross Church,
boy did we celebrate!

CHAPTER TWO

BACK TO YOUR ROOTS

It's now coming up to seven long years since the closure of our beloved church of Holy Cross. The time it hurts most is when one of the parishioners, past or present, dies, that's when the reality well and truly hits home once again.

I'm sure most people's last wish is to return home to their roots in preparation for their final journey. I sadly remember the first Holy Cross funeral, which took place at Saint Anthony's on Scotland (Scottie) Road; soon after the closure of our parish church. There we were waiting outside the church, Holy Cross parishioners, past and present.

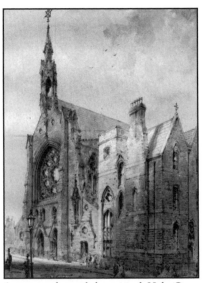

A water colour of the original Holy Cross Church which was described on opening as a mini cathedral because of its interior grandeur. The building was created by the renowned French architect Edwin Welby Pugin.

Once again bitter tears are shed as the loss painfully hits home we have no parish church to presently call our own.

Josie Kelly one of the oldest parishioners of Holy Cross with such sadness in her eyes remarked, We're like gypsies travelling around the City in order to pay our last respects. It seems so unjust when we had lovingly built two beautiful churches, one destroyed by enemy fire, the second sold off to the highest bidder to eventually build on the site a block of luxury apartments.

One of our beloved and still revered O M I Fathers Father Tony had travelled to celebrate the Requiem Mass, as he stands proudly on the beautiful altar of Saint Anthony's he clears his throat, he too found it hard to compose himself.

His opening line while scanning the familiar faces in the congregation here celebrating Julia's life it breaks my heart to see you all here, once again holding on to the break in his eloquent voice, continuing on I too know how you are all feeling this day.

As it was also my parish church where I grew up? Hankies, at the ready sobs were stifled discreetly. Father Terry quickly stems his own emotions to embark on a pleasurable nostalgic trip down memory lane, to evoke the magnificent traditions that helped create the parish of Holy Cross to be ever renowned and revered throughout the parishes of the Archdioceses of Liverpool.

I can honestly sympathize with other parishes like us who had the heartache of losing their Churches. In the Inner City over the last few decades it seems we have suffered most Holy Cross, neighbouring parishes, St Mary's Highfield Street, St Joseph's Grosvenor Street. The Friary Fox Street, also St Gerard's and St Alphonso's. Saint Bridget's and not forgetting All Souls both were demolished to make way for the new ring roads all once proud parishes steeped in their own distinctive and individual traditions, once vibrant and thriving.

Sadly over the decades the heart of our city has been virtually ripped out causing an exodus of city dwellers to the outskirts of the city, that meant falling numbers in the churches that where once were full, the community's having been reluctantly shipped out to the new towns. It has to be said these newly formed parishes were greatly enhanced by the arrival of the "townies" yet never forgetting their inner-city roots.

Just recently an old friend and neighbour of Fontenoy Gardens died, John Cross who was a loved and respected lad, who at the tender age of 21 years was left in charge of his younger brothers and sisters, after the premature death of both his parents. The Cross family were a large one consisting of ten children.

The way, in which he took over the mantle, he was indeed a credit to his deceased parents. He earned so much respect from the older generations of the Gardens in the mature manner he shouldered his new responsibilities. Unselfish with his own personal time, he cared for the younger members of the Cross family. John was 58 years of age when he died, he fought his terminal illness with so much courage and dignity. It was at Saint Matthew's Church, Queens Drive, where John's family and friends celebrated his Requiem. Once again it was the meeting of the Holy Cross clans. It was mentioned in Father Connors sermon about John's life, in which he remarked to the overflowing congregation, that in his first ever conversation with John after Sunday morning mass was to ask whereabout in the parish he lived.

John Cross a proud Holy Cross lad.

John replied with so much pride, Oh I'm not from around these parts Father I'm originally from Holy Cross, Father Connor who hailed from Northern Ireland had only recently arrived at Saint Matthew's. He spoke of how aware he was of the passion openly displayed by Liverpool people, so fiercely proud of their parishes were they had firstly originated. Back to their roots so to speak.

There always was a fierce yet healthy rivalry between neighbouring parishes, because (at the end of the day forgive me *please* for using a footie cliché) most of us had close relations that originally (that word again) who had hailed from those neighbouring parishes many decades ago. Weird how we still up to this present day ask on meeting people, that same old question? What parish are you from *originally*, how quaint don't you think? No I don't think so it's your roots, your heritage, all of which you proudly and lovingly cling on to for as long as you can.

So many people who have purchased my first book kindly informed me, I'm not from your parish but my Grandparents were, and instantly reminisce about the fabulous outdoor processions, along with their own precious memories of the splendid times we once shared in the old neighbourhoods.

Sadly another friend and neighbour of 'Fonnie oy' passed away recently, not long after John, Lily Morgan nee (Burrass) both her and John were diagnosed with the same illness shortly after one another, together they attended healing masses, keeping one another's spirits high, when each so badly needed it. How brave they both were in sickness, together they kept their faith glowing, renewing them both bodily and spiritually, Lily attended her friend and neighbour Johns funeral knowing in her brave heart that her couragous battle to live was dwindling every minute. Yet here she was in attendance to celebrate John's life, looking a million dollars as usual knowing full well time was fast running out for her. At Lily's wake there was plenty of stories from the Auld Neighbourhood, how we love strolling down that familiar place called Memory Lane. Lily's Requiem Mass was celebrated at St Johns Kirkdale were she had lived for over 28 years. Relocating after her home in her beloved Holy Cross was demolished. Father McSweeney stood on the altar quite amazed at the sheer numbers that had packed the church, so much so they had over spilled out in to the street. In his eloquent tones he welcomed everyone in the congregation, so charmingly too. 'So today is the gathering of the famous Holy Cross Clans'. To pay our respects and sing in unison to the good old-fashioned type hymns of yesteryear in which we can passionately sing our hearts out to. In remembering of what we had and how much we have lost in the past decades. We will however try and hold on until it's our turn to say our farewells and finally leave the building!

Father McSweeney mentioned in his sermon, that a parishioner of Saint John's, Margaret Donnelly had written a wonderful book about the noble and illustrious history of Holy Cross parish. (My goodself) he was graciously reminded that she was a Holy Cross girl before Saint Johns, he chuckled at the prompt but friendly reprimand and graciously added that he will rephrase that statement, Margaret is originally from Holy Cross, which I silently thought Yes as it was In the Beginning And Always Shall Be. As the saying reads, you can take the girl out of Holy Cross, but you can never ever take the Holy Cross out of the girl, you better believe it! Both John and Lily had truly wonderful send offs, both richly deserving for their good turns in life. John for his dedication in looking after his loving family.

Lily Morgan was a proud
Holy Cross girl.

Lily too for her kindness in helping the homeless and less fortunate people who through drugs and alcohol had fallen by the wayside.

Lily tried in her own special way to make their lives a little better, always with a smile never a moan, how dignified she accepted her illness. The Holy Cross Clans gathering as always in their own unique and special way in order to pay their last respects, to two dyed in the wool Holy Crossers.

May They Both Rest In Peace, Amen.

CHAPTER THREE

DO YOU REMEMBER?

Can you remember those old-fashioned local shops, usually situated on the corner of every cobbled street in our city of Liverpool? The familiar smells you always and ever associated with those particular type shops. We had a few such shops in our community, especially the chandlers shop. Lily Orford owned the chandlers on the corner of Bispham Street; on walking into the shop all kinds of different cleaning smells hit your nostrils, like bottles of 'Aunt Sally' disinfectant, firelighters, paraffin; familiar childhood aromas, which somehow stay with you forever. I can close my eyes and picture still to this present day the variety of colourful pictures on Lily's walls advertising various washing products, Lux soap flakes, and Colemans Dolly Blues all contributed in achieving a whiter than white wash.

Lily Orford was such a gentle person, I can picture her still garbed in her ill-fitting navy blue 'Wetherall' overall. The shop was quite higgledy-piggledy but ask Lily for any item under the sun and Lily knew exactly were to locate it.

Enamel buckets, carbolic soap, and those huge scrubbing brushes with different size bristles protruding from the rough wood. Donkey stones, or sand stones one of the same, white or brown, all of these items were top sellers. I really can not remember any mops on sale, it was down on your hunkers scrubbing hell out of floors and stairs, such hard work, but in those days the belief was cleanliness was right next door to Godliness, you better believe it!

Browns the dairy and shop was situated at the top of Alexander Pope Street, they sold not only dairy products but also gorgeous fresh cream cakes. The shop was pleasantly presented tiled walls and floors ever so bright and spotlessly clean; our teachers often sent you on errands for bottles of gold topped milk, and a box of fancy cakes, that event only ever occurred of a Friday.

I can remember if you were chosen to wash up the dishes after break, as a reward you were given any of the cakes that had not been eaten.

Sadie Carol's was situated at the top of Alexander Pope Street, Sadie had several different colours of red in her hair, 'dyed to dollrags' the older customers would whisper while waiting to be served, as Sadie's shop was adjacent to our school of Holy Cross we kids popped into Sadie's on the way to school when we had a spare penny to spend. Those old time favourites, pear drops, pineapple chunks, Uncle Joe's mint balls, Walker's toffees, and creamy Holland toffees, weighed on the scale and poured into the small triangle bag. You received a square white bag if you were purchasing a quarter of sweets (which was very rare). Having to produce your allotted coupons was a pain as sweets were still rationed long after the war was over.

SCHOOL FUND RAISERS

You did not have to be reminded that Christmas time wasn't too far off when the gift envelopes arrived for the blind children. On the front of the envelope was a picture of a beautiful little girl with short curly hair. Her face looking up to the sun, her eyes closed. The picture and caption made you feel so grateful, so in turn you wanted to donate all your spare pennies. On the back of the envelope there was a festive picture of Santa holding a sack, the sack contained small divided boxes, in which you entered a cross when you deposited the penny. The sack had twelve boxes if you completed all of the boxes the total in old currency amounted to a half a crown.

You felt so benevolent; when filling in the boxes, a visit to the Gaiety cinema was forfeited to enable you to fill Santa's sack. Remember the Good Shepherd Fund, this fund was to benefit the poor waifs and strays, and this particular fund commenced at the beginning of lent and finished after the six weeks of lent.

Each class had a chart in the shape of a thermometer, shaded in meticulously every week according to the amount, which had been donated. Each week the amount was steadily rising. When delivering the registers to the other classes our class teacher would instruct me to clock how their class chart was shaping. Thinking back now to those years, down the line, it was a wonderful ploy by one of our favourite teachers Miss Haynes, to encourage us to contribute that little bit more. She was quite a psychologist on the sly.

The Good Shepherd Fund was handsomely supported as every other good cause was in our more than generous community.

FIRST HOLY COMMUNION MEMORIES

How over the decades times can change so drastically, for instance Holy Communions. My God, the preparations now are almost on par with arranging a wedding. A venue is booked months before the event, also a children's entertainer, don't forget the DJ, a lavish buffet of hot and cold food. In the centre of the table stands a cake in the shape of a church or a bible open to reveal the name and date of the Holy Communicant. Believe me when I say this I'm in no way knocking these celebrations as my own two gorgeous grandchildren Katie and

My first Holy Communion
Photograph taken
at Jerome's Studio.

Sarah they too had the works. It is one of the most important days of your life receiving the Blessed Host for the first time. Sadly the Religious side is now put in the shade by the 'over the top' after festivities. Our First Holy Communion day in contrast was oh so different. I recall we had to fast in those days from the night before. The morning couldn't arrive quickly enough. Gazing at your Communion outfit hanging on the wardrobe door ready for the big occasion, made your head whirl with excitement, a white dress with a long white net veil and to complete the ensemble was a white pair of shoes and white ankle socks. A shiny backed prayer book and pair of mother of pearl rosary beads. You were absolutely delighted, usually a present from your godparents.

I can remember gazing into the long mirror of the mahogany wardrobe in the bedroom, my hands clasped together so very angelic. I was allowed for that one special day only, to wear my long black hair loose, I was lucky having been blessed with a good thick head of hair, which luckily had a kink too, it, looked quite nice loose. My other mates were not quite as fortunate as me; they had to sleep with a head full of rags entwined around their soaking wet hair to produce a head full of curls, to capture the look of the glamorous American child star Shirley Temple.

Such agony endured but that's the price to pay baby in order to produce a mass of glossy curls.

My lovely school friend Angela McGinn had no such problems her 'woolly' head of curls were natural no dreaded rags for her to suffer. There was always a few 'conk outs' boys, as well as girls who through lack of food and drink fainted, one of the teachers with the help of one of the Young Men's Society swiftly carried the casualty into the porch of the Church for a whiff of fresh air.

Sometimes this was more of a hindrance than of a cure. Adjacent to the entrance of the church was the brewery; the smell of the hops made you want to vomit even more. The lads too were dressed 'up to the nines', for the special occasion, smart navy blue serge suits, white shirts and ties. I somewhat felt the girls received much more attention than the boys on this wonderful occasion. Suppose it was more obvious because the girls were completely decked out in white from head to toe. After the ceremony we were taken home to enjoy a hearty breakfast after a drink of water, first and foremost. Later on in the day we were hawked around to close relations, and friends and were generously mugged (not the same definition these days I'm glad to say)

Shoppers called to you in order to press a coin into your hand as this gesture was deemed to be lucky to the contributor. I was delighted counting my donations.

On the following Monday morning dressed once again in my

Communion ensemble, we met for assembly in the school hall. The tables were prepared laid with the usual party food, jelly and custard, marshmallows, sausage rolls. The Parish Priest was in attendance to present us with a certificate of Our Lord with the Apostles at the Last Supper. The inscriptions beautifully written in bold copperplate writing.

Which read: This is to certify that Margaret Gildea celebrated her First Holy Communion at Holy Cross Church Fontenoy Street. This was our makeshift Church as our own beautiful church had been destroyed in the 1941 May Blitz in which our City of Liverpool had taken a terrible hiding from the might of the German Luftwaffe.

Jerome's photographic Studios, London Road.

A trip to Jerome's photographic studios in London Road was the highlight of your life. I still have the photograph, my Mam had it lovingly framed in an Art Deco type frame. It hung on the wall in pride of place in our tenement flat at 33B Fontenoy Gardens until my brother John reluctantly had to leave our once happy family abode. Were we so happy and content living amongst the best friends and neighbours, you could ever wish to meet the "salt of the earth".

We were so lucky in our community surrounded by hard working people, so genuine in their friendships, generous to a fault. My God how blest truly we were, those vintage friendships have stood the test of time continuing up to this present day. Still on the Communion theme, my good friend Tommy Kelly was reminiscing the day of my book launch when afterwards we called in for a drink at The Poste House in the city centre. Tommy recalled the day his sister Mary took him to Jerome's studio in order to have his photograph taken in his Holy Communion garb, he recalls looking (the gear) as he was perfecting his pose the fussy photographer instructed him to smile directly into the camera, Tommy being the bold child that he was pulled a face.

His sister Mary had paid up front for the portrait. The photo was promised for the following week. Mary awaited the bold me laddo to arrive home from school to accompany her to the studio for the photo. Tommy was not that keen, I wonder why?

Mary could not wait to see the photo when she took one look at the photo; there was the imp posing but not a very flattering pose. He knew he was in for it so he scarpered pronto out of the studio. Mary was not too far at the back of him, he recalled every time she looked at the photo he got a belt around the ear, she was furious with him, 'one and sixpence that cost do you realize that' she shouted angrily, another reign of slaps reigned down at Tommy's head, he finally managed to dodge away from Mary into the Picton Library for his own safety.

Tommy Kelly reluctantly posing for his Communion photo

When he finally reached home his other sisters Joan and Sally gave him the rounds of the kitchen. Once again he feared for his own safety he ran quickly to his Nins, a safe haven as he thought, faking the tears he sat on the fireside chair, Nin was beside herself having witnessing one of her favourite grandsons in floods of tears, visibly in shock. She huged him comfortingly into her flowered pinny inquiring who was responsible for all the tears, threatening what she would do to the culprit if she came across them. Tommy's tears soon subsided when his Nin produced a big doorstopper (a piece of bread cut nice and thick loaded with his favourite strawberry jam). As he wired into the buttie his sister came rushing in to show his Nin the offending photo. After the conversation in the kitchen Nin was now witnessing the bigger picture so to speak, she calmly walks over takes the half eaten buttie off Tommy and declares 'You ungrateful little article one and six wasted muttering every auld clichés under the sun, the famous chestnut of them all like, money not growing on trees. Once again he was given the rounds of the kitchen, ministered by his Nin too. He couldn't believe all the commotion over a blinking photo, which he did not want taken any way, how we laughed. I can't wait to see the offending photo can you?

On seeing the so-called offending photo, (I honestly think in my humble opinion of course) that the Kelly family was bang out of order 'kicking off' on Tommy, in fact I think it's dead cute. The little angel! Don't you?

DOMESTIC SCIENCE

Tuesday morning was our weekly cookery lessons. Now politically correctly renamed home economics, we girls really looked forward to this period. Walking in two's up Bevington Bush where the lessons took place.

The building in fact was part of Saint Bridget's school; across the playground was the school clinic. As we entered the classroom, which was really cold first thing in the morning, whether it was summer or winter making you somewhat reluctant to shed your warm coat.

The classroom was huge, housing cookers, tables were scattered around the classroom at strategic points, and two pupils each shared a table. I felt so grown up attired in a crisp starched white apron, which covered the front of your dress, a white starched cap sitting quite jauntily on top of your head secured by two hair clips we were raring to go. Our first couple of lessons was quite boring; we were taught first and foremost, how to prepare a room for a good cleaning.

There was a partition separating the living room from the bedroom we were instructed how to correctly sweep the floor, making doubly sure the corners were well brushed.

The next procedure was to kneel down on the wooden floor equipped with an enamel bucket of hot sudsy water, a rough piece of carbolic soap. A scrubbing brush as big as a corporation sweeping brush. Standing directly behind you the teacher constantly checked your progress, urging you in a loud authoritative voice to apply more elbow grease, my hard faced mate Angela McGinn would cheekily raise her hand and request a tin of elbow grease. A quick flick of the floor cloth across her backside alerted the rest of the pupils not to be so bold. We really did have some great times at domestic science lessons. Our next chore was to apply floor polish which smelt heavenly of lavender, very liberally spread on to the floor, shortly afterwards vigorously polished off with a clean soft cloth. The next lesson was the making of a bed, tucking in the corners (hospital corners) the sheet neatly turned down over the cotton counterpane. I was glad to see the back of the vigorous cleaning regime, but looking back it was great fun.

The following week we were instructed to provide a white pillowcase, as we were taught the art of perfect starching, how to iron the perfect starched pillow case, as stiff as a board! How we giggled. At long last the day arrived for our very first cookery lesson, bring it on!

Ingredients consisted of a large spud, a quarter of red mature cheese, and a small onion along with a firm tomato to garnish the top of the spud.

Kitted out in our spotless white pinny and cap (which we had designed at our sewing class) we were ready for action. We really did feel quite grown up, in fact the blinking bee's knee's.

Linking arms with your classmates we walked the walk up 'the bush', armed with a white enamel plate required to withstand the heat, trimmed in navy blue.

The ingredients secured on the plate by a checkered tea towel. We were eleven years of age, our first year in seniors, here we were our first cookery lesson, learning the basic art of simple cooking.

The art of learning to cook was sometimes, well I suppose was absolutely hilarious; my Dad was the only one of my family who would dare sample my culinary delights. Devouring even the disastrous dishes, he always encouraged me. His favourite sweet dish was apple crumble. I eventually became quite a dab hand at the crumble delight smothered in Monks custard (the gear).

The best time for me at cookery lessons was the preparation of baking a Christmas cake; it took almost three months to complete. The list of ingredients seemed to go on forever. We had to provide a round tin box in order to keep the bun loaf part of the cake fresh so as to soak the sherry up. The next stage was adding the marzipan.

How hilarious was that procedure, my mate Mary Lawrence had almost eaten her packet before we arrived. Talk about the icing on the cake! Really there was some serious calamity's on the way, again by my mate Mary, she had piled that much icing on the cake our teacher remarked it did not take that much ice to sink the titanic.

On hearing that comment we both collapsed in to fits of laughter, much to the annoyance of our tutor.

I was designated to help Mary by the furious tutor because I had found the incident so amusing. We practically had to chisel off the offending icing; it took all of two weeks to make it look even half decent. The lessons did not as I recall discover a budding Nigella Lawson or a Delia Smith, looking back (there was quite a few calamity Jayne's) the lessons were a welcomed break from the boring every day learning of Math, English and other mundane studies in the classroom, we took domestic science as license to have a bit of harmless fun.

A festive frill purchased from Blacklers helped disguise a multitude of sins; a few plastic cake decorations, a snowman, a Christmas tree and a little red-breasted robin completed the Christmas scene. I was quite pleased with my effort, truly I was. In fact couldn't wait to show off my creation. I was delighted with the 'ooh' and 'arh's when I finally presented my work of labour. Until I overhead my Mam remark to our next door neighbour Tess Riley, 'It had been cheaper at half the price Tess if I had ordered one from Fortnum and Mason' who ever they were!

Do you remember the Christmas carollers, [bloody pests] a couple of weeks before Christmas, we'd descend on the residents of Fontenoy Gardens to warmly serenade them in our word perfect voices. Weeks of practicing in school with our music teacher Miss Haynes meant we were really up for it. Accompanied by my best mates Mary Donnelly, Vera Curran, Kathleen Silker, Ann Bernia, Angela McGinn, we began on the first landing of our tenements, our repertoire well planned.

First carol sang was Silent Night, Good King Wenceslas, followed by Adeste Fideles, we boldly rapped on the knocker with a rousing rendition of, Christmas Is Coming, *The goose is getting fat please put a penny in the old man's hat, if you haven't got a penny a ha'penny will do, if you haven't got a ha'penny, well god belss you!* There was another ending, the lads used, but as we were ladies we never stooped to their derisory chorus! I'm sure you will fondly recall their bawdy rendition.

When the door was eventually opened nine times out of ten we were richly rewarded, especially on Thursdays and Friday nights as they were pay days [we weren't soft] we knew the score.

Sitting on the stairs of our tenements we shared the spoils, afterwards taking ourselves off to Chiappes' chippy. To treat ourselves in good style to a fish and chip supper accompanied by a glass of cream soda. The season of goodwill had certainly arrived early for the carollers' of Fonnie-oy Gardens.

Christmas time in the tenements were really magical, our flat was decked out in gorgeous coloured festive decorations all the stops were pulled out to make it a special time especially for the kids. There was always an abundance of rich festive food, as our resourceful Mams had saved a few bob each week in the various local shops, guaranteeing a heaving table throughout the Christmas holiday.

CHAPTER FOUR

SPECIAL MOMENTS, GRAND TIMES. GROWING UP IN FONTENOY GARDENS

Fontenoy Gardens was situated just a stones throw from the city centre of Liverpool, a large prominent block of art deco styled tenement dwellings. I was born and reared at 33B Fontenoy Gardens spending the best days of my life, amongst a vibrant and close-knit community.

Looking back, I suppose to a stranger visiting our community those blocks of tenements must have looked quite daunting, especially after the war, when looking out on to a huge monstrosity of an air raid shelter practically dominating the centre of the tenements.

It stood as a reminder too, as that monster prevented many a resident's death after enemy bombs rained down perilously on the parish of Holy Cross. The air raid shelter became famous throughout the city as a landmark for an annual religious pageant, which occurred during the month of May.

From every part of the city people travelled to witness a very beautiful and poignant ceremony, the crowning of our blessed Lady's statue right there played out on this ugly brick shelter. The shelter was transformed for the religious occasion.

The first procession took place after the war and attended by hundreds of people including a large contingent of American airmen. Who were at the time were based at Burtonwood near Warrington. They were enthralled at the sight unfolding before them, never having witnessed anything quite like a Holy Cross May procession.

One of the officers filmed the spectacle, knowing he had just witnessed an unusual event, which he felt would capture the interest of the world. He dispatched the film off to America. A few weeks later the footage was beamed around the world on the popular Pathe worldwide newsreel! The rest is history as they say Holy Cross famous May processions captured on camera to be seen in all their pomp and ceremonial glory by a worldwide audience.

Besides having to endure an ugly old shelter, we also had a set of [what we kids called the belly irons] these cast iron railings were a boon to us kids providing us with many happy hours of playing the game of gymnasts. To the kids of Fonnie-oy they were a means of many happy hours of playing. In our own little fantasy worlds we became world-class gymnasts, after enduring many strenuous hours of practising intricate moves balancing on the top of the railings. The belly irons were a set of cast iron railings, which were directly in front of the ground floor flats of the tenements, in our square of Fontenoy Gardens.

At the end of the railings a set of stairs were attached to the entrance of the flats. It was during the school holidays especially, when we amused ourselves for hours on end. The lads also joined in the gymnastic game too, ably showing off their delicate skills. Attired in suitable black canvas pumps which enabled you to confidently balance on the narrow bar, with a quick sharp turn, arms outstretched taking time to compose yourself, one, two, three you're on a roll. After a bit of a dodgy turn your confidently back in control, concentrations now spot on. It's show boating time one foot in front of the other brimming over with confidence continuing in an exaggerated show off style to the end of the bar. Skirts checked and securely tucked under the tight elastic of the leg of your knickers (not very lady like). Jumping ever so deftly on to the concrete below with the most elegant of style and grace of an Olympic well tuned gymnast at their very best. Quickly whipping your skirt down from under your knickers you'd graciously appreciate the enthusiastic applause from your mates sitting patiently on the edge of the kerb waiting eagerly for their turn. In order to perform a bit more magic. You'd really think we were performing in an Olympic stadium competing for a precious gold medal instead of a delicious jam buttie from an appreciative on looking neighbour.

It was much easier for the lads to perform as they were far better attired than we girls, donning a pair of short kecks, a pair of pumps they were ready to go. We had some right show offs in Fonnie-oy, the lads especially, as they always loved and ever had to go one step better than the girls, which nine times out of ten ended up a cropper, needing a visit to the Northern Hospital with a suspected broken limb! Such show offs, Such Happy Days.

A great view of the famous Belly Iron's were we spent many happy hours walking the walk showing off, many broken limbs were recorded in Fonnie-oy but what joy we had strutting our stuff 'On the Belly Irons'.

SUMMER HOLIDAYS

In those difficult hard up days we knew how hard it was for our parents having to make ends meet and we really did appreciate when one of our benevolent neighbours volunteered to take us along for a day at the seaside via the lanny, (Pier Head) what a palaver it was in arriving there safely, in itself a miracle! Walking down Tithebarn Street, passing St Nick's Church, (known as the sailors church). Proceeding on walking towards the overhead railway, another quick head count is taken, no stragglers, all heads are accounted for the signal

A view of the three graces on a crowded ferry crossing; how the passengers dreaded the mass invasion of us kids running up and down the decks intruding on their leisurely cruise across the Mersey.

is given by Annie Moran and off we go continuing on our journey. Marching quickly yet walking quite cautiously, across the dangerous floating bridge. My brother Jimmy by this time is causing mayhem as he perilously swings to and fro swinging on to the thick metal chains, almost ending up below in the treacherous murky waters of the River Mersey.

Already waiting in the queue at the ferry terminal are our other close neighbours, the Kennedy's, and further on joining the back of the queue are the Bernia family; pandemonium once again breaks loose after yet another quick head count is taken. Finally it's all aboard the ferry, to cross the River Mersey. Good news filters through to the Fonnie- oy crew, the tides out so we decide to settle and park our selves on the sand. Shirts off followed by our shoes and socks. It's an almighty dash into the sea; squeals of delight fill the rich salty fresh air. Each and every one of us delighted in enjoying a sunny day at the beach. Life really is a bowl of cherries especially today with the sun shining so brilliantly on our little milky white bare backs.

Feeding time, was always and ever an hilarious scene, Spam butties, a couple bottles of Corpy tap water, which contained a dollop of sherbet, after a quick vigorous shake, the bottle was then swiftly passed from one to another, swigs all round, you just had to craftily work the head and make doubly sure you wasn't on the last swig, as there was always a fair chance that alien objects were floating around! When you were dying of thirst it really did not matter that much, the lads played footie, while the girls, collected crabs in a rusty old tin bucket.

We meticulously channelled the sand into five or six lanes, enabling us to race the crabs. What laughs we had it was sheer bedlam once again when the time came to depart for home locating missing socks, undies, ribbons, as well as tempers, all just a tiny bit frayed around the edges, due to the effects of the blistering sun. Leaving for home at the same time was always a race against time as our Mams had to report for work before five o'clock!

I loved being late, for it would result in a ride home on the 44D tram, the grumpy conductor wasn't too pleased though. Quickly we'd dive upstairs out of sight away from the hawk eyes of our Mams. For a little bit of a carry on, the flustered conductor is now in a real tizzy not knowing what kids belonged to whom. Quite a few went awol when the conductor arrived with his ticket machine it was a serious game, a crafty battle of wits, but I can assure you all quite a few of the little fonnie-oy darlings bagged a free ride home courtesy of Liverpool Corpy transport. Kids will be kids after all wont they? Especially after a baking hot day in the sun, when one and all were just an itsy bit on the hyper side.

The 44D tram what a treat for us kids to ride home usually we had to walk. A Penny well spent meant we had a ticket to ride all the way home.

Upon opening the front door the most gorgeous and inviting smell of a cooked beef casserole still simmering in the oven, famished after spending an hectic day in the fresh healthy sea air, believe me you'd have gratefully eaten a scabby cat (As My nanny Woods would have

31

said) my sister Mary quickly tidied the table, ready for my Dad's arrival. We kids were soon off out again to play in the square, reliving the brilliant and most enjoyable but quite a tiring one too, after a few hours the sunburn slowly appeared, with a vengeance, there was some terrible whining that night, believe you and me.

The solitary bottle of calamine lotion purchased from Banners the local chemist was bandied from one flat to the other, in order to cool and soothe the kid's scorched skin.

Isn't there always a price to pay after an eventful and wonderful day? How times have changed when a small bottle of Banner's pharmacys watered down calamine lotion being the only known cure in order to cool down the precious little angel's scorched skin!

A DAY OUT TO MORETON

Moreton was another favourite summer destination for the fonnie-oy gang, I loved our our early Sunday jaunts to Moreton .We travelled there by train, I hated the walk off the train to the seafront it seemed an age until we finally arrived at our destination. After settling down, it was time for a game of water footie in the sea. Once again feeding time, total chaos reigned as usual. Eating our lunch on the sparse grass, my Mam purchased a pot of tea from the catering van, just a little further up another van was doing a roaring

The Holy Cross lads posing after a dip on a day at the seaside and a bag or two of the best Juicy cockles in the world.

trade in selling chips. How delicious did those greasy chips taste when plonked on to your corned beef sandwich so tasty. My Mam and her neighbours being ever so tidy minded helped clear the debris after lunch. Time once again to send for another jug of hot water, to top up the teapot for one last cuppa. We had all the time in the world today as it was Sunday, great not having to return home early especially for our Mams, which was an added bonus. The best time of the day had arrived the tide was now way out; we are ready for some serious cockling duties.

We carried quite large canvas bags in order to transport the cockles home. The Holy Cross crews were working away, eager little beavers, quickly filling the bags. Under strict orders to choose, only the larger of the cockles, discarding the smaller of the crop. Experienced and well versed in the art of cockling, time had once more stolen upon us.

Another sunny day captured on a brownie camera.

It's time to head home to catch the last train, but not before enjoying the gorgeous sight witnessing the setting of the Moreton sun, the late afternoon sun slowly slithering down as if in slow motion from the red now illuminated sky how we cheered looking back now presently I declare it really was a heavenly sight! Returning home was likened to a military styled operation, as the kids were reluctant as ever to leave behind, the setting sun on Moreton beach. We were all so plum tuckered out after the really arduous graft of cockling managing only just to keep our tired little peepers open, as we tiredly walked to the train station for the journey home. Approaching home to Fonnie Oy you suddenly had a surge of bounding energy maybe the thought of a fresh brown Hovis buttie heaped with warm freshly cooked cockles, accompanied by a pinch of salt and lashings of malt vinegar, sheer unadulterated bliss when the big fat juicy cockle burst in your mouth the most delicious taste ever, of fresh seafood, to tantalize your taste buds. The kids of Fontenoy Gardens were indeed connoisseurs when it came to the art of cockling. ***Simply the best!***

MAKE DO AND MEND AFTER THE WAR

Reminiscing as usual at one of our countless reunions I love recalling how we kids happily played for hours on end on the bombed hollers thousands of bricks lay scattered across the waste ground were once stood neat rows of terraced houses, part of the wrecked houses still stood, a tragic reminder of the terrible loss of life in one terraced street in the parish. Playing house we girls collected the full bricks creating a living room, a bedroom, and a kitchen, how resourceful we were, tables strategically placed in the centre of the room, of course created out of bricks. In the centre of the table we placed a jam jar containing a bunch of yellow and white pee the beds (weeds). We girls amused ourselves for hours on end, carefully collecting the different coloured glass which was buried amongst the piles of rubble, such fabulous colours in rich reds, greens, blues and amber. My close friend Joan Jeffers informed me that the glass was from a specialized workshop, which had made stained glass windows for churches and the posher establishments in the more affluent parts of the city. Building a shop along side our houses we used the different coloured glass as currency to purchase our fags (sweet cigarettes) such vivid imaginations as we played out our imaginary games on the 'holler'.

Childhood fantasies played out so seriously on a bombed out waste ground, building and creating kept us occupied for hours on end. Until the lads arrived, alas they too were playing out their make believe game Cowboys and Indians. Armed with sticks, oops! Sorry I mean Winchester rifles riding invisible horses wildly. Looting our houses and shops, screaming we try to head them off but to no avail. We were a trifle peeved but not for long, as it was time to head off home. All part of the game of mend and make do, compromise, we were good, in fact past masters, happy knowing tomorrow was indeed another day to play and again re-build another abode, to wile away the time.

How resourceful when shortages were still around many years after the war. Collecting spilt brown sugar from the Tate and Lyle motors, scooping the sugar from the cobbled street into a tin, no thought of hygiene, only of the thought of making toffee back at our newly built house. Creating a fire inside the bricks we placed the tin of brown sugar, taking turns to stir the mixture, impatient to wait until the mixture cooled down, we'd then share the spoils sitting comfortably in our make believe world, looking back, how happy and content we were in making do with a hundred weight of resourcefulness!

CHAPTER FIVE

THE EVACUEES

My sister Mary was one of the many children to be evacuated to 'Betws-y-coed' in Wales. By attending Fazakerley open air school the pupils were sent away much earlier than the rest of the evacuee's. My sister Mary had suffered with a congenital heart disorder. Both my parents were devastated at her early departure; much later there was a mass exodus of Liverpool children to Wales. There are many lovely and touching stories to be told, but sadly so many ugly ones too, which are more akin to horror stories, of vulnerable underage children who really did not know what was happening in all the confusion of war.

Kids of Holy Cross who were evacuated to Wales.

Mary soon settled into her beautiful surroundings in the heart of the Welsh countryside. Within weeks she had shot up in height and was presently looking the picture of health. She had quickly got used to the countryside and very soon began to recognise every plant and flower by name.

My Mam and Dad tried their utmost to visit as much as they possibly could. I can recall Mary remembering when the teacher called her name to inform her she had visitors from home, running through the corridors and actually seeing your Mam and Dad when sometimes it could have been as long as a month. She could not contain her feelings throwing her arms around them both, and at the same time contemplating the contents of the brown paper carrier bag.

When it was time to depart, it was the most terrifying feeling in the world, thinking of the one worst possible thought, that you may never ever see them again.

Not seeing her friends too was awful; as they had been fortunate to be billeted together but in another part of Wales. Mary was dying to see her 'landing mates' from Fontenoy Gardens. Patsy Kennedy and her sister Teresa, what a wonderful surprise when they unexpectedly turned up accompanied by their Dad who was home on leave from the army.

Mr Kennedy was in uniform he was a sergeant, such a very handsome man. The teachers sneaked to the visitor's room just to have a peep at the handsome man in uniform. Mary was absolutely thrilled at having her two friends visit her; they could not believe how big she had grown, and how posh she now spoke in fact 'dead posh'!

It was on a return journey home from the war zone to Liverpool in which Mr John Kennedy's plane was attacked by enemy fire causing him to lose his young life; he was thirty-three years of age, leaving behind a young wife and four children. Many more Liverpool men and women were to lose their lives in the bitter and savage conflict of war.

John my older brother's story thankfully was a very happy one; he was such a big child that he was always mistaken for being much older. When our parish of Holy Cross took a direct hit, the decision was quickly taken.

Mr John Kennedy.

More children were to be evacuated immediately for their own safety. John was not quite four, but quite easily have been taken for a seven year old. Along with hundreds of other children he was hauled off to the railway station, my poor Mam was beside herself with grief, after waving off yet another of her precious children at the same time hugging her oldest son John, who really was not too perturbed, in fact he was quite excited at the thought of a train journey to another country.

Carrying his small brown attaché case, along with his Mickey Mouse gas mask, his name label securely attached to his coat lapel he was more than ready for his adventure. How sad must that scene have been, to distraught parents waving off their kids into the unknown? My brother John spoke often and fondly about his time with his adopted Welsh parents, Mr and Mrs Jones in Llangollen. The Jones's never intended to house any evacuees. John recalls the worst time in his young life, after the realisation hit home that when he reached his destination, he was not returning home to his beloved Liverpool and his family, he started to wail. Immediately being advised to shut up as a big lad like you bawling, you will have all the younger children howling. Little did the warden know that John was the youngest evacuee present? He still remembers it as the worst moment in his young life, feeling he had totally and wholly had been abandoned by his parents. Together they were horded into the village church hall; he recalls the scene, absolute bedlam, children screaming unmercifully for their Mams and Dads. Carrying out the strict instructions issued beforehand to them by their parents. The message related was to stick together, especially brothers, sisters, cousins and friends. Upon being selected by the villagers there was even more chaos, the kids from Holy Cross were adamant and would not budge one inch without their nearest and dearest! Poor John was now left on his lonesome, witnessing the kids he grew up with being carted off screaming and kicking, yet he was the only one left, probably because he too was still howling, everyone had given him a wide berth! Left sitting alone on a battered old chair, with his worldly belongings at his feet, talk about 'Nobody's child'. Starting to whinge once again as he was so bewildered, as to this little, or suppose I should say a 'big lad'.

Even more confused when the officials started to blather away in their own native tongue, wondering what time they would eventually get their own weary heads down, they still had the last scouse whinge to dispose of that being John Gildea. He was once again taken into a van to be literally hawked about the village, but to no avail, till divine intervention stepped in.

The van stuttered to a halt, after much swearing under his breath the warden summoned John out of the van. The warden banged on the door of the Jones's, they were an older couple who were childless, they had both made it clear to the authorities they were not interested in having any evacuees at any cost.

The warden took no heed he banged even harder. Mr and Mrs Jones appeared in their bed attire, opening the door wider, in the gloomy shaft of light the Jones's caught their first glimpse of John Gildea, cold tired and very vulnerable, the tears once again cascade down his pale and tired face, and very nearly down his 'kecks'. He was desperate for a visit to the bathroom.

Mrs Jones extended her arms inviting this dishevelled Liverpool urchin into them. John did not hesitate he remembers clinging on to her, that was the moment John Gildea crept in to their benevolent hearts.

After a cup of cocoa accompanied by two welcomed pieces of golden toast, he was shown to one of the spare bedrooms, tucked in by the kindly Mrs Jones were he slept soundly till ten o'clock the following morning.

On waking and almost forgetting his ordeal of yesterday, he glanced out of the bedroom window to witness mountains and trees and even more trees, the sun was shining down enhancing the breathtaking scenery. John was suddenly awash with the worst feeling of total loneliness God love him;

The bedroom door slowly opened and there they stood his *newly adopted Welsh parents*. They invited him down to the warm and cosy kitchen for his first meal in his new abode. After breakfast John was given a tour of the house, feeling much better and a trifle more secure John was to remain with the Jones's who in a short time loved him like he was their own son, not having being blessed with children of their own both felt John was sent to them as a blessing in disguise.

Stan was a carpenter by trade, he created so many fabulous wooden toys for John, slowly but surely this little Holy Cross urchin was slowly beginning to fall in love with the Welsh countryside, as well as basking in the lap of luxury. Fontenoy Gardens in war torn Liverpool was slowly fading from John's memory. My Mam and Dad along with the baby at the time, my other brother Jimmy, managed a trip to visit John, just to ease their minds knowing exactly where their son was now safely domiciled.

John's happy abode during the duration of the war

The Gildea family arrived at the front door were Peggy and Stan eagerly awaited them, John was quite shy and somewhat withdrawn, until the Jones's discreetly left, in order for them to spend a few precious hours together once more as a united family. My distraught Mam cried for the rest of the journey home. John did not show any emotion what so ever on their departure.

My Mam threatened to return and take him home there and then, but my Dad knew that's all it was a show of bravado deep down Mary knew her son was in capable hands; please God this cruel war may soon be over. John had now grown even bigger, and dressed so beautifully. The Jones's had a recent photo of John displayed on a small mahogany table beside the fireplace; this infuriated my Mam even more. She felt in her heart he was becoming more their son than hers. Peggy gave my Mam two copies of the recently taken portrait. My nanny Woods kept her copy under a glass dome where it remained until her death. She loved that particular photo of her eldest grandson remarking at the time that he looked a real little Lord Fauntleroy, God bless his little cotton socks!

As the war drew to an end, John was still lovingly ensconced with the Jones's, my Mam was expecting a baby (that was me) she had been so ill during this pregnancy, being admitted to hospital the doctors fearing she may not carry this child full term. John remained with the Jones's having no idea there was another sibling on the way. John visited home accompanied by his guardians, who were truly lovely and caring people, and it was quite clear that John was now the centre of their world. They both sat down and discussed with my Mam and Dad if there was even a remote chance of them both adopting John after the war. I don't think it's printable what my Dad's reaction was. The thought of his son and heir, his namesake, and here were strangers wanting his lad. Running to Mr Jones, John began to bawl requesting to return home. The scene left my Mam and Dad heartbroken, my Dad deciding that the time was right for the return of little Lord Fauntleroy whether he liked it or not, he was homeward bound, sooner than later.

After I was born my Mam was so ill, being laid up for weeks on end, my nanny Woods was now practically living with us, cooking, cleaning, washing, she kept the home ticking over.

A visit from the Parish priest, with a timely reminder it was now time for John to return home. He was almost eight years of age and still not received his first Holy Communion. My brother John recalls his homecoming as really weird, when Mr Jones parked his car in the square of Fontenoy Gardens, the kids came flocking around the posh vehicle to see who was alighting from the car.

My Mam told me the tale years later; I also had John's version too. John sadly recalls the day he arrived home with a brand spanking new suitcase filled to the brim with his beautiful wardrobe of clothes, along too came the hand made toys his pride and joy. There was a scooter, a three-wheeler bike, a beauty with bright silver mudguards, and a large shiny bell on the handlebars. My Mam recalls welcoming those two wonderful people welcome into the family home. The table was laid with the best china and the Sunday posh tablecloth, it was an awful atmosphere my Mam recalls John sensed he was being abandoned again for the second time, but this time by his adopted parents, and was reluctant to leave their sides. When the time arrived for the Jones's to depart the scene was totally horrific for both parties. John was hysterical screaming, he had to be physically held down by my Dad, still he continued to cry for the two caring people who had lovingly kept him safe through out the war, they loved him like he was their own son, John at that moment felt he belonged with them. Mr Jones practically carried Peggy, his broken-hearted wife down to the car. Finding Johns scarf on the seat of the car, he ran back up the four flights of stairs, a good enough excuse to give John one last hug before returning home to Wales. The kindly Mrs Jones had recently knitted John a scarf and gloves, for the winter. Both of them had patiently and lovingly nursed him through his early childhood illness, and now he was gone, given to them through a war, but always knowing deep in their Welsh hearts, John was only ever on loan.

Reluctantly they returned him back to his roots, which realistically they knew the right time had come.

John's version was much of the same, recalling the terrible moment in his life, when he knew his time in the Welsh countryside was slowly running out. It was time to return to a city that had been ravished by German bombs. When he finally did arrive back to his abode in Fontenoy Gardens it was almost a total culture shock for John. He remembers inquiring earnestly were his face flannels and towels were kept and which bedroom was he to occupy.

We only had two bedrooms, my Mam and Dad in one bedroom (with me in the same bed), my sister Mary in the other bedroom sharing with my other brother Jimmy. He remembers sobbing at the thought of not having his own bedroom, and the view he presently had was of a huge ugly air raid shelter dominating the centre of the tenements. Welcome home to the real world kid! Sobbing lying on top of the bed, thinking he'd never felt so wretched in all of his young life, pining for his Welsh adopted parents and the green, green grass of his Welsh home! Jimmy his younger brother annoying John constantly by requesting 'a go' on his three-wheeler bike. Jimmy took the bike delighted at that moment with life, cycling wildly along the landing at a great pace. Till he tried to manoeuvre the bike around the tricky turn in to the 'ally oo' (balcony at the end of the landing) he did not have a clue how to apply the brakes.

The next performance he went careering down the flight of concrete stairs. He was pinned in the corner with the bike wrapped around his face, our nearest neighbour was Mrs Kennedy, she picked him up, terrified as his face was completely covered in blood. His eye was almost closed, he was screaming saying he could not feel his eye. He was promptly carted off to Saint Paul's eye hospital post haste. Where he was detained until the following day where he underwent an exploratory operation to discover the extent of the damage. Gladly his eye was saved, gradually the injured eye returned to normal after a few weeks. The fabulous three wheeler bike was banished to the veranda, were it lay till it eventually rusted away, my Mam forbidding any of us to ride the cursed bike ever again.

John later returned to school at our local parish school of Holy Cross, were after a few weeks was assessed at being at least three years ahead of his age. He remembers vividly the way he was being 'skitted' for the way he spoke and also his superb manners. Given a few weeks John had his old mates all around him, bonding didn't take long, he was accepted back again into the community were really he had rightly always belonged. I can honestly say though that his posh early upbringing remained with him through out his life. He always walked so proudly, shoulders back, head held high, and spoke really nice, well I thought so.

Only a few years ago, John felt he wanted to revisit were he had spent his early childhood during the Second World War. He booked into a bed and breakfast for a few days, in order to take a long awaited, nostalgic walk along that familiar country lane. He was really shocked on walking into the village newsagent for his daily newspaper, instantly the old lady recognised him. You haven't changed one bit you are Mr and Mrs Jones's little treasure. John said he was really gob smacked after all these years; she went on to update John on all the comings and goings in the village. Especially about the whereabouts of the Jones's, sadly they had both passed away. Their house had eventually been sold; John felt so sad and bitterly regretted not having kept in touch. The following day he visited the local cemetery to recite a few prayers for his caring Welsh Mum and Dad who were both so kind and generous with their love when he was most in need.

John visited the house knocking on the door explaining to the new owners who he was and the purpose of his visit. Both were really gracious towards him, immediately inviting him to join them for afternoon tea. After tea the new owners gave John 'carte blanche', to take his time and explore what once was his adored home. Sitting on the bed in his old bedroom, gazing once more through the window at the scenic view, the view he awakened to each morning, during those long dark days of conflict. Instantly recalling all the wonderful times he shared in this still very beautiful house, but most of all he could still feel the love, in the house, so privileged, to have shared precious time with two special people, who had loved him so dearly. In time John had grown to love his adopted parents with all of his heart. The new owners informed John that his timing in coming to visit the house was indeed lucky, as they were planning to change the whole look of the house both internally and externally. Very kindly they sent John photos of the house just the way John would always remember, where he had remained safe and sound, but most of all loved for the duration of the war.

I called into see my good friend and old neighbour Tommy (Golly) Gallagher, he gave me so many evacuee stories, again some not printable! But so humorous that I will savour and use at another time. If you knew Tommy personally you'd appreciate my comments. One of towns great characters, we enjoyed whiling away many hours reminiscing about the treasured times we enjoyed in our parish of Holy Cross.

There is to this day the same pain at the outrageous decision to close our church, especially now as the celebrations of the 800th birthday of our City of Liverpool approaches. The pain is still raw and my heart truly goes out to other parishioners who too had to endure the sadness of losing their parish churches.

Tommy loved recalling his time in Wales or as he refers to his evacuation as being (turfed out to Wales). There is a photo of the Holy Cross crew taken when they first arrived in Wales. Within five minutes of their arrival an accident occurred Joe Concannon fell and broke his arm, up to six families were housed in one large house, to the kids, at that moment in time they thought of it as being one long adventure.

As if they were on holiday, at the back of their minds this lark was going to be over in a few weeks. How wrong they were for it dragged on and on and on.

Tommy was with his older brother Pat, and his younger sister Bibby, as Christmas was drawing near they tried their best to make the house look festive. Tommy recalls his older sister Maro arriving with a new outfit of clothes for both him and Pat and his younger sister Bibby for Christmas day.

There was plenty more were they come from. A real effort had been made for (the poor kids in Wales). Old wool stockings filled from top

to toe with familiar festive fayre of nuts, tangerines, Fry's chocolate bars, the bottom of the stockings contained a few 'thrippny- joeys'. Tommy being the cheeky and resourceful imp he was (and still is) managed to confiscate all of Bibbys share of the thrippny-Joeys.

Christmas morning arrived on waking the first thing the kids did was attack the Christmas stockings. Under the difficult circumstances the kids had done extremely well as there were chronic shortages of every conceivable item. Tommy was quite pleased with himself, until he witnessed his sister Bibby's crestfallen face.

At that precise same moment his older sister Maro entered the room immediately noticing the distressed look on her younger sister's face, she knew right away who to point an accusing finger at. Tommy knew he had been well and truly rumbled.

Maro with as much diplomacy as she could muster explained to Bibby how Santa had been somewhat confused in the blackout mistakenly depositing her share of the money into Tommy's sock.

With the delicate situation solved, Tommy received his just rewards, receiving a good 'clout' across his lughole! In his own words he explained that he really came unstuck for his obnoxious actions, causing every Auntie who visited during the holiday, to administer their disgust, at his selfish actions he said I got battered! Deservedly so!

I must reveal though that he carries a serious guilt complex still to this present day.

He can still vividly picture his sister Bibby's sad crestfallen face.

Punishment is still presently being served. I'm sure you would agree. Tommy's sister Bibby entered the Carmelites Order (Sister Mary of the Angels), suppose you could say that our parish of Holy Cross have been more than a trifle generous to the Ministry, we also have Father John Cullen, Father Terry Murray, and Father Denis Parry who is currently serving in Peru.

May God keep him safe?

Pat Gallagher, Tommy's brother recalls his stay in Wales as an evacuee at the time quite daunting, but after half an hour on seeing the amount of trees with an abundance of apples it did not take him long to enjoy the fruits of the earth!

Suppose the arrival of the boisterous Liverpool inner city kids to a quite and most picturesque village in Wales truly must have been quite a culture shock for the village people. One such person was a retired headmaster residing in the same house, as the evacuee's from Liverpool. Mr Hughes was not the least pleased on their arrival to noisily shatter his idyllic retirement.

He was constantly chasing the boys from the orchards warning them not to eat the apples, as they were not edible till another further few weeks.

The boys did not heed Mr Hughes advice branding him as the village worst moaner. How they wish they had heeded his warning later that same day after eating the forbidden fruit the evacuee's were writhing in agony with chronic stomach ache. The village Doctor was hastily summoned to the house his diagnoses, sour apple belly. Their guardians apologised profusely, but genuinely were worried in to thinking that their little darlings had been purposely poisoned. There were quite a few misdemeanours to occur, the worst and yet the funniest was when the lads decided to reinact a cattle drive, just like their hero John Wayne from a classic cowboy movie.

The lads could not believe how many cows and sheep were grazing in the meadows [not for long though]

Ray Black [boss drover] decided they'd round the cattle up and head for the centre of the market town. The day they chose for the drive was the busiest, market day. Utter chaos reigned as the cattle ran amok, the inexperienced crew along with Ray at the front impersonating his cowboy hero the one and only 'Duke', John Wayne. You can now imagine the carnage unfolding, yet the kids from Holy Cross was hell bent on enjoying their first cattle drive what an adventure for the city kids, head them up and move them out!

Maybe for John Wayne 'cos they certainly were not moving in the right direction for wanna- be- boss- drover Ray Black.

As expected there was a deluge of complaints from the neighbouring farmers demanding the instant removal of the notorious evacuee's from Liverpool?

Mr Hughes surprisingly stepped in to the fray to defend and plead for mercy for the 'wanna-be cowies'. As the weeks passed Mr Hughes and the Holy Cross cherubs struck up a fragile truce in fact Pat recalls quite a serious bout of bonding began after news reached them from the village.

It was Mr Hughes who had championed their cause pleading for them to be given one more chance; his plea was successful yet somewhat grudgingly granted.

Mr Hughes had come out of retirement and began to tutor the city children; he taught them in both Welsh and English. After a few weeks the children were singing harmoniously in the Welsh lingo. Quite an achievement they did not have a clue what they were singing about but none the less Mr Hughes was elated by their speedy progress. Over the months Mr Hughes and the children grudgingly at first but hasten to add they both began to show a serious affection for one another. Respect quickly followed on as Mr Hughes now looked forward to the daily lessons especially as their Welsh lingo was now blossoming, quite a feather in his [Welsh] cap. Mr Hughes became friendly too with the children's mothers respecting them for their ingenuity, their resourcefulness in cooking exceptional meals with so meagre rations. He was always included on the meal rostra, which he was eternally grateful. Pat was a little anxious this particular morning as Mr Hughes was already five minutes late for class, which was so not like him; he was always set up well before the children arrived.

Deciding to go and investigate Pat quickly walked around to the side of the house were Mr Hughes resided he knocked quite sedately on the first knock, no response, giving the door a fairly good bang yet again still no response. Pat peered through the bedroom window he could see clearly that the headmaster was lying in the bed. Shouting his name and continuing banging on the window to no avail. Pat was seriously worried now for the headmaster's well being. Raising the alarm he summonsed the ladies who opened the door quite easily their suspicions were founded. The old teacher had peacefully passed away in his sleep during the night. These studious and no nonsense type ladies from Liverpool set about preparing Mr Hughes to meet his maker.

He was swiftly washed and shaved with the utmost care and sensitivity, changed into a clean night shirt Mr Hughes was now presentable to not only meet his maker but to the mourners from the village who'd visit to pay their last respects. While changing the bed linen and turning the mattress, the ladies discovered a colossal amount of money; summoning the appropriate authorities the money was collected for safekeeping.

The ladies were commended for their integrity and trustworthiness indeed Mr Hughes had amassed a fortune in money the amount later revealed was over seventeen thousand pounds quite a fortune in the year of 1942.

Mr Hughes was now ready for the influx of visitors, the first as to be expected were the Holy Cross urchins solemnly paying their respects to the Welsh headmaster who over time had become their friend. The feelings were indeed reciprocated by their old once grumpy teacher. Pat recalls fondly his wartime memories of the time spent in Wales and still remembers to this present day the Welsh lingo especially on hearing hymns. He quietly reflects why they were despatched in Wales in the first place yet they enjoyed their adventure they were the lucky ones surrounded by their own kith and kin. Eventually to return home to their beloved City of Liverpool, none the worse for their hilarious exploits in the beautiful Welsh countryside.

CHAPTER SIX

QUEEN OF THE ANGELS
AND QUEEN OF THE MAY

I t was in the year of 1932 when my sister Winifred was born; it was a cold and frosty February morning when she bawled her way into the world.

Nurse Reagan the local midwife announced above the racket there was certainly nothing wrong with her lungs. From the moment she opened her eyes, the parish of Holy Cross knew she had arrived. Winnie instantly alert after the commotion of her birth, her beautiful blue eyes studying each and every one of them in turn. The kindly neighbours remarked that she certainly been here before, as she continued to study their faces so intently for a baby of scarcely minutes old.

The supportive neighbours as usual were on hand to tidy around and make a welcomed cuppa, while also attending to my other sister Mary, who was still only a toddler herself until my nanny Woods arrived to take over the reigns.

My Nan had just obtained a new flat in Birkitt Street; these newly opened tenements were being hailed as luxury flats. Suppose to the new tenants they were mansions, as most of them had been living in the most antiquated Victorian dwellings, sharing toilets, kitchens with no running water facilities. They were some of the worst slum and rat infestered housing in the City of Liverpool. I can recall my Mam telling me how delighted they were when my nanny finally moved in to 68a Birkitt Street.

The new raved about flats were situated in the parish of St Mary of the Angels of Fox Street, also known as The Friary, as the parish was run by the order of the Franciscan monks. The kitchen was equipped with a deep sink, hot and cold taps, a gas boiler, a good size living room, two bedrooms, and the pure sheer luxury, of a bath and toilet. My Mam and Dad was still living in a flat described as a cockloft, as it was a top floor flat, one living room, and one small bedroom with a kitchen as small as a postage stamp.

The tenants shared a toilet at the bottom of the stairs. Like all her neighbours they fought so very hard in order to keep their homes spotlessly clean. This new arrival of theirs was so different from my Mam's first born. Mary was so quiet, and also a very sickly child for the first few years of her life. Winnie was just nine months old when she began to walk. My Dad was delighted with his little live wire of a daughter. She was the living image of him, jet-black hair, and piercing blue eyes, a trait inherited from her Irish ancestors.

My Mam lovingly told me of how she became an adored and somewhat feisty little character amongst the residents of Adlington Street. She loved visiting the neighbours especially the older ones, who she loved to entertain, as long as they were feeding her and spoiling her rotten. She never ever showed in stature for all she ate, my Mam describing her as *'not as big as two pennyworth of copper'* My Dads family met up every bank holiday at my nanny Gildea's at 34 Bispham Street they'd have a fine auld time, my grandparents had a large backyard, where they housed a donkey, known by the name of Spanish Jack who helped to hawk the fresh fruit out to the outskirts of the City. The family being of Irish origin was a very clanished family, the cousins who had moved out to the outskirts of the City, returned to their former parish of Holy Cross in order to party!

The party commenced to the sound of accordions, banjos, penny whistles; a rollicking good time was had by one and all. Winnie especially, she loved the family gatherings my Uncles Jimmy, Paddy and Eddie adored her, the more they swung her around the more she loved it. She loved to dance to the music her dainty feet tapping to the music; my Dad's older nephews Jimmy and Willy Carr tossed her high up in to the air, the higher the better for this little minx. Her one burning ambition was to take part and walk in the annual May procession, especially the outdoor celebration.

The terraced houses were gaily decorated for the occasion with paper buntings and flags strewn across the streets, from one house to the other. Winnie appeared with one of my Auntie Cissie's best lace cream curtains ceremoniously draped from the top of her head almost reaching to her dainty toes. Her hands dramatically clasped together her eyes half closed so piously, lifted up to heaven. Her sweet little voice singing her favourite hymn, Oh Mary We Crown Thee, she had difficulty in sounding her letter R's and my Mam recalled that her impediment made the hymn sound even more poignant. Winnie eagerly waited for the day when she too would be dressed up to the nines, to join the other infants in procession, walking around the streets of the parish. Winnie celebrated her fourth birthday, two weeks before Christmas; how she loved visiting her beloved Auntie Cissie's where she was absolutely doted on. Her older cousins were home on leave from the Royal Navy, as soon as she opened the back door they'd pounce on her, throwing her from one to another. Her excited squeals echoing through to the parlour were Auntie Cissie was sitting in her wheelchair. As usual she'd severely reprimand her two sons warning them 'you're going to do some serious damage to that precious child one of these days the way you both man handle her'. The more they swung her the more she loved it.

This wild child was indeed the apple of their eyes. They could also tantalize her too, especially Jimmy he loved to wind her up, she was wearing her new winter coat, which she had modelled for them earlier on, walking up and down the backyard twirling this way and that way. It had fur trimmed around the collar and the cuffs how she loved her new stylish posh coat as she referred to it, until Jimmy whispered in her ear, Winnie's got a coat with s__t around the collar and s__t around the cuffs. Well that derogatory remark about her new coat was all it took; she kicked off howling and bawling, the tears rolling down her face. Jimmy was mortified and tries his utmost to pacify her, as one by one the neighbours appeared at the front doors to inquire why their favourite child was crying. He'd try to bribe her with a trip to the Lannie, (Pierhead) but she wouldn't wear him not after ridiculing her gorgeous new coat. She could quite easily switch her affections to Willy, who'd be delighted. Winnie never fell out for long with her handsome cousin Jimmy, especially when a promised visit to the

Lannie was once again on the agenda.

Jimmy deposited Winnie back safely to the tiny but cosy garret, Winnie being totally tired out. After a quick dolly in the kitchen sink, she'd then snuggle up in the old worn out easy chair in front of the inviting coal fire. Not before relating what a great day she had spent in the company of one of her favourite people in her life. Jimmy reluctantly slipped away to meet one of his many adoring girlfriends. Winnie then remembers the episode about her coat and what Jimmy had cruelly said, so she relates in her baby way to her doting Dad every sordid detail. Whispering the swear word, in his ear, her Dad feints disgust threatening to run over to his house and take his belt off in order to leather Jimmy with it.

This threat delights the tired Winnie; sleepily Winnie informs her Dad that he won't be home, he will be in Mick Walsh's (the local pub) with his new girlfriend. So to hang fire and wait till tomorrow then tackle him, how this little cherub had the ability to make every one around her laugh.

Winnie loved to skip from one house to another especially during meal times. My Mam would be really vexed with her because she would have already eaten her tea. Leave her be my Auntie Cassie would say, she needs fattening up. Winnie loved to share in her great Auntie Cassie's tea, dipping into the tomatoes and bacon gravy with a huge chunk of crusty bread. She never did grow any fatter with all she ate.

At the time there was quite a serious epidemic of diphtheria in the community; two children from the bottom landing in the dwellings had recently died. There was so much grief around at that time in the little block of flats in Adlington Street. My Mam as usual was always available to offer a kind and helping hand. It was such a different scenario when a child passed away, than an older parishioner, the wake was more sombre, a little angel, too good for this wicked world, was the comforting condolences whispered in to the ears of the heartbroken parents.

In times of trouble friends and families rallied around, especially when there was no insurance money available. Such hard times but seen through by generous benefactors, whom didn't have much themselves but always contributed no matter how small the contribution. God love them. Constantly willing to give what they could ill afford. It was this closeness that generated one of the most clanished communities of that impoverished era. Winnie had not been too well; complaining that her throat was hurting, she became very lethargic, and her face had become very red and swollen. Doctor Connolly the local general practitioner was hastily summoned, such a kind and generous man who too was a great patron to the surrounding communities and not just to our parish of Holy Cross.

This wonderful and dedicated Irish Doctor was always available day or night to attend the poor of the parish. He seldom took his fee, leaving it discreetly under the saucer after a quick brew, how immensely grateful the people in the Vauxhall and Scotland Road area. Were to this wonderful dedicated Irishman and his wife too who, unselfishly served their patients? His children carried on the Connolly dynasty right up to this present day at their surgery on Commutation Row.

The Dr's Connolly are remembered and revered still with lasting gratitude and affection. Doctor Connolly had his worse fears confirmed, he suspected Winnie had more than a sore throat, he advised hospitalization immediately.

Winnie was diagnosed with the dreaded disease of diphtheria, at the Northern hospital where she was so ill practically choking to death. She was holding her own for a few days, the one thing keeping her alive was the thought of achieving her one longed for ambition to take part in the May procession. Her bespoke outfit proudly hung in the cupboard waiting. A pristine white dress with an enormous bow, a wreath of white roses to crown her 'sticky out' veil, white buckskin boots, she was elated.

Auntie Cissie was described to me as a very strong and straight talking woman, yet she was reduced to tears when Winnie so serene walked in from the parlour decked out in her May procession attire, like a little angel almost floating, so innocent.

Her gorgeous Irish blue eyes shone in sheer delight.

She did the rounds of the parlour walking slowly as my Mam and Dad, along with her older sister Mary looking on so proudly. Auntie Cissie and her two favourite men in her life stood beside her and sang together like they never sang before.

Oh Mary we crown thee with blossoms today Queen of the Angels and Queen of the May. Winnie was in her element delighted as usual in being the centre of attention, she was then very reluctant to take off her pretty May procession outfit. Many years later my Mam stated how she treasured that poignant yet happy scene throughout her life seeing Winnie in her May procession outfit.

Winnie's short life was now slowly ebbing away, my Mam and Dad never leaving her bedside. As she was such a well-loved little character around the parish, the close neighbours in the flats were distraught. This petite little girl was presently in the Northern hospital fighting for her young life. A miracle was not to be, she died peacefully in the arms of her broken-hearted parents. The local undertaker arrived from McDougalls to break the disturbing news informing my parents Winnie was to be allowed to rest at home for one night only, they were the strict instructions issued from the hospital authorities. The tiny coffin would sadly have to be a closed one. My Mam and Dad were distraught; my Auntie Cissie was beside herself.

She had a word with the undertaker, asking for his valued advice.

If there was any possible way they could gaze on her tiny angelic face, maybe just for one last time.

He pondered for a while, then suggested a small glass concealed in the lid, which would enable everyone to say his or her last goodbyes to this beautiful little angel.

They agreed and that certainly helped ease their pain. At least they'd have her home again, to gaze upon her impish cherub face for at least one more night.

My Mam spoke often in the later years of her life about my sister Winnie whom I'd never known. How she was so loved by friends and neighbours who on that bitter cold February day (just a few days after her fourth birthday, patiently queued along the landings and down the narrow staircases, filing past the tiny coffin to pay their last respects, to this vivacious little girl from Holy Cross. Who's one and only wish was to wear her gorgeous outfit and take part in the most famous of all May processions in her Parish of Holy Cross. Her outfit was graciously donated to one of Winnie's little friends who proudly wore it to walk around the decorated streets of the parish and remember her best friend Winifred Gildea, who was most certainly now an angel, in heaven, and probably singing at the top of her voice, "*Oh Mary we crown thee with blossoms today Queen of the Angels and Queen of the May*"

DÉJÀ VU

Many years later my own daughter Lisa, was too elated, when the time arrived for her to take part in the May procession back in the early seventies.

The May processions were not the extravagant affairs they once were in our parish of Holy Cross. The crowning was now taking place in the confines of the church. The crowds still travelled to witness the wonderful and beautiful ceremony of the crowning of the statue in the centre of the main altar. When Lisa appeared in her pretty white dress carrying a posy of fresh flowers, my Mam's face became almost mask like. I could not speak because I thought she looked so pretty standing posing in the middle of the living room. When I noticed the tears rolling down my Mam's face, unchecked I could not utter one word. Our next-door neighbour Tess Riley stood rooted to the spot; she too was crying openly declaring she looked a picture of innocence.

Tess began to kiss her face so gently as if she was seeing an apparition.

Lisa was lapping up the attention twirling around to show off the effect of her dress.

My Mam still could not find her voice. Lisa, my Mam truly believed was her daughter Winnie reincarnated because of the uncanny likeness and her every action. She stood on the rug in front of the fireplace and began to sing in her sweet, but slightly out of tune voice. 'Bring flowers of the fairest'. She sang the hymn word perfect just like another proud little Holy Cross girl many years before her. Standing in the pew of our beloved church of Holy Cross. I linked my arm through my Mam's squeezing her arm as together we sang our favourite hymn witnessing once again the crowning of Our Blessed Lady. A Holy Cross occasion carried out in the same grand traditions of our late and proud ancestors. Memories once again renewed, flooding back to the glorious May processions of yester- years, when the streets of the parish were crowded, how sad that a beautiful Catholic tradition is no more. Thankfully we still have in our possession the sepia photographs to treasure and mull over, to pass on to future generations. Catalogued in an album of loving and treasured memories of the way we were back in the golden years of a parish steeped and blessed in unique traditions.

As long as the bowers are radiant with flowers we will continue to treasure those glorious occasions celebrated on a dreary air raid shelter. Let us not forget that same shelter safely protected the residents of Fontenoy Gardens for the duration of the war. In thanks giving every year after the war the statue of Our Blessed Lady was crowned by the May Queen, to a packed auditorium in Fontenoy Gardens during the summer month of May.

P S

I've included a procession photo of my daughter Lisa, because when my friend Rose scanned the original photo a circle of white surrounded her head, which certainly was not present on the original copy, I'd like to imagine maybe my sister Winnie was actually walking beside her during the procession that proud day as my daughter fulfilled her young ambition on that sunny May day.

My Daughter, Lisa

Queen of the Angels and Queen of the May. Oh Mary We Crown Thee

*The buntings and flags are out flying once again in celebration
of the crowning of our blessed Lady's statue.*

*The first May procession after the war years took place on the air raid shelter in the
centre of the tenements. This beautiful service was recorded by an American airman
leading to the historic event being beamed all over the world via Pathe News notice the
amount of people taking part along with the throngs of people viewing.*

CHAPTER SEVEN

GOLDEN MEMORIES

Of course they had to originate from Scottie Road! This meeting genuinely was the scenario when I first met up with Pat and her husband John. Pat's family had originally hailed from Saint Bridget's parish. After a good old gab as per usual about the good old days. Tommy my better half let it slip that I had written a few stories for the prestigious Irish magazine 'Irelands Own', Pat thought what a wonderful achievement, so too did the waitress.

In writing my first book, I was truly overwhelmed by the amount of cards and phone calls, which I had received. Thanking me for taking the time to write My Parish Holy Cross.

Letters arrived from all over the world. Expressing how on reading the book, helped to refresh their golden memories of the past. Not only ex-parishioners, but also from surrounding parishes who were only willing to share their memories.

Some are not printable... or well maybe at a later date!

Here's one I chose because it is a favour long over due being called in, fair exchange no robbery as my Auntie Maggie used to preach.

I met Pat on a trip to Ireland were we were staying over for the New Year period. We met by being allocated the same table for the duration of the holiday. Typical scousers as soon as you sat down, before any formal introductions are made, your asked 'What are you having to drink'. I always maintain Liverpool is akin to a village every one knows somebody's sister or brother, or they had once worked together such a small world. The waitress arrived with our drinks reminding me of the famous writers including George Bernard Shaw, W B Yeats, and Samuel Beckett all three winners of the Nobel Prize for literature. My claim to fame is I write for the 'Scottie Press' our community paper and truly proud of the fact. Pat was now fully convinced that I really was a fully-fledged author, I wish!

As the mead flowed Pat constantly talked about her Mam and how she really was a well-known and popular character from the Scottie Road area.

Nellie was a one off always described as a real get up and go character. Not one to let the grass grow under her feet you may say. If there were a good opportunity to forge ahead Nellie would exploit it.

Pat promised me a collection of treasured family photographs of the many momentous religious occasions and events over the decades from the parish history of Saint Bridget's. The deal was struck I was to write an amusing story about her Mam (which indeed is fact) and include it in one of my books. Pat stuck to her part of the bargain; mailing the wonderful photos to me.I have to agree with Pat they are truly magnificent, capturing our heritage in its simple beauty and nobility of our Roman Catholic faith. Indeed of even more valued as the changes in our city and communities have changed beyond recognition. Thanks Pat.

THE RAT CATCHER

The Second World War was now inevitable; the signs from Europe were not favourable. The media predicting it was only a matter of time and the Country would engage in war against Germany. Our men were slowly but surely leaving key jobs all over the city, in order to fight for King and country. Women were fast filling the jobs that were left vacant by the men of the city.

The council were advertising vacancies in the cleansing departments, street cleaning, and janitors the 'corpy' was severely depleted. Almost in dire straights as the city was having a grave problem with not only the invasion of Germans but rodents too. The position was a well paid one.

Nellie was browsing through the situations vacant section in the local paper. 'The Liverpool Echo', had reported that there was an acute shortage of pest control officer's posh description really as in reality they were advertising for rat catchers. Nellie being a very resourceful lady read the advert with interest. Like most of her neighbours Nellie was struggling to make ends meet, so too was her younger sister Betty. Nellie decided that they would present themselves at the Municipal offices in Dale Street, first thing Monday morning.

Nell's sister Betty was in no way as enthusiastic as Nellie her go-getter sister was, in fact she was horrified at the thought of catching any type of pests, she was terrified of spiders for God's sake never mind sewer rats. Oh my goodness what was she letting herself in for, but knew she would in the end tag along as she was in no mood to discommode her older sister Nellie. Monday morning arrived much too quickly for Betty's comfort, Betty feigned a sudden bout of tonsillitis. Nellie was not swallowing that poor excuse from her dithering sister, have a good hot strong cup of tea advised Nellie.

Betty eventually made her self presentable after a quick once over by Nellie, Betty was given Nell's approval, 'you look really nice, you suit blue, should wear it more often girl' said Nell. Betty was quite chuffed by Nell's compliment. Very rare she gave out compliments, but quick to comment when she thought 'you looked a show'.

Over a cup of tea Nellie once again persuaded Betty to be a trifle more enthusiastic at the interview, think of the plusses not the minuses was Nell's advice. Betty felt sick at the very thought of trapping and eventually killing the rats. A cold shiver ran slowly down her back, Nell noticed the change of heart immediately in her sister by her body language, Nell suggested that she herself would take on the daunting task of catching the pests. She would only expect her to tie a bow at the top of the sack. How's that for a compromise. Your good at bows aren't you girl said Nell with that comment they both took a fit of the giggles.

Presenting themselves at the Municipal offices of the Council, they were given a card stating their interview time. It was an afternoon appointment. Betty sighed with a sense of relief. Nell suggested a leisurely walk around the town centre and indulge in some window shopping. It was soon time to return to the office, Nell had planned to arrive in plenty of time for the interview.

Nellie was brimming over with confidence knowing in her heart she was going to be successful she had a good feeling in her bones. Giving her young sister a quick sideways glance she was not as confident for her chances. The friendly commissioner approached the girls explaining that they were running late.

Asking would they mind being interviewed together as they were sisters? Nellie thought this was another good sign, whispering to her terrified sister to leave her to answer the questions. Betty felt a load had been taken from her shoulders. More than happy to let Nellie take charge as always.

The girls were shown in to the office by the same commissioner, he whispered good luck you'll need it. He's one surly individual, adding in a somewhat shady voice and he really can't stand women either.

For the first time Nell's confidence wavered just a tad after hearing that timely info. The surly being invited the girls to sit down directly in front of his highly polished desk. Introducing himself as Mr Jones he gave the girls permission to speak, what a pompous being he was thought Nellie.

Mr Jones took off his spectacles and began to polish them vigorously with his crisp white handkerchief, his initials boldly embroidered at the corner of the hanky. Adjusting his glasses he is quite confused for the minute in thinking the girls were present, interviewing for the office cleaning jobs. Nellie quickly puts him straight were here for the pest control vacancies. Without further ado Mr Jones commences with the interview, a smug smile slowly spreading across his pug face.

Leaning back into his rich ox blood leather chair, he asks in a sarcastic manner, which he was well noted for especially when dealing with women. Exactly what experience have you two women had at catching rats, indeed a loaded question? Mr Jones presently feeling even smugger adjusted his glasses waiting for Nellie's answer. Nellie quietly cleared her throat and in a clear strong voice pronounced *we're married to two rats!* What more experience is required answered the bold Nellie Purcell. Mr Jones for once in his life was at a loss for words he fell across the desk in a fit of raucous laughter and could not stop the tears. He mopped his eyes announcing loudly. You both start your employment at half past seven Monday morning sharp! You have quite made my day my dears, said Mr Jones. What an outrageously funny story to unfold at the wife's next dinner party.

This story epitomizes the strength and unique sense of humour that we scousers are born and truly blessed with.

Nellie at work setting the trap.

Nellie Purcell was to be the one and only ever woman 'rat catcher' in the city of Liverpool. Nellie was born in 1910 and attended school in the Scotland Road area and was one of nine children. Nellie was proud of her roots and proud of her Irish heritage. Nellie was a well-known character in Liverpool and in 1945 the local newspaper 'The Liverpool Echo' published a story about her time spent as the 'rat catcher' recording on camera the capture of her 500th victim.

After the war when the men returned home Nellie did not step down from her position in fact she was promoted to the position of senior training officer such was her outstanding record, she later became a health inspector for the Vauxhall area.

MEMORIES IN A CAPSULE

Last year I had the privilege of attending a project arranged by the students of Liverpool Hope University, the intention was to capture various sepia photos depicting the way of life during the early days of parish life. Fondly trading memories with the older residents and sharing their special moments of how they had lived and survived during the worst bombings of the Second World War. What games they played, how their childhood compared with the modern era up to present day.

The collected information of memories and memorabilia were to eventually be placed in a time capsule to be buried in the garden of remembrance, by the schoolchildren were our beloved statue of the Pieta now stands proudly in Standish Street. The memories were indeed a pleasure to once more mull over and once again treasure, remembering the horrendous happenings of the Second World War.

Yet when listening to the older generation of Holy Cross who as usual made light of the situation, choosing to remember the laughs and not dwell too long on the cruel and senseless loss of life. A bombardment of continued air raids almost wiped out part of the Holy Cross community. Tears shed openly once again for the many children of the parish who lost their lives through an epidemic of the killer virus diphtheria.

The senior generation briefly made reference to the horror side of the war, when a bomb dropped dead centre in amongst a row of terraced houses totally wiping out a generation of vibrant family life. What sadness having to witness eight coffins of varying size in the parlour of a small terraced house, containing men, women and children laying along side each other, a family united in death, casualties of a senseless war. Annie one of the mature parishioners quickly diverted the discussion to lighter memories of her childhood when seeing the students were visibly moved by their personal experience and horrific memories of the war.

The students recognize Annie as a true Liverpool character, a good storyteller, encouraging her to recall the games she played as a child. Annie needed little encouragement she took centre stage; not realizing her every word is being recorded for prosperity and pride of place amongst many more in the time capsule.

Annie's ever-alert eyes lighting up, when she mentions her grandmother. Annie lived with her grandmother, explaining at the time she was all of seven years of age. When she began to read to her in her childish pronunciation of difficult words. Her eyesight failing, Annie became her grandmother's eyes pausing, to explain to the students that she really was a little 'auld' woman for her tender years.

Annie's gran had nothing but praise for our American Allies, who generously donated food parcels which contained the famous, but humble tin of Spam. Annie fondly recalls the culinary expertise of her Gran and how she successfully managed to invent a dozen different ways to serve up a slice of the tasty Spam! Annie remembers clearly as if it was only yesterday the presence of the GIs in and around the parish during and after the war. Loving once more to speak and inform the Hope University students about life in the early days of the parish and how it grew in stature. Recalling how she first met her husband, later working as an extra on a movie set along side the famous Hollywood movie diva Barbra Streisand. Nothing fazed Annie; the students were enthralled, loving sharing in her memories of latter years with them. My favourite one is this little gem in which I will sign off with.

Annie loved accompanying her Grandmother, as well as reading to her, and travelling with her, especially by train. Annie read every railway hoarding to her Gran that was displayed on the station walls. Annie read that colourful poster to me my girl, the one advertising the tin of Spam and the handsome American soldier, her Gran asked.

Annie took a deep breath, as some of the words were a trifle alien to her. Annie began words to this effect, The poster began, 'Beware! As our allies may leave more than a tin of Spam behind, be cautious and aware of the disease in brackets (VD)'. Gran paused a while after Annie read the advertisement digesting the info for a minute or so then replied, "Well Annie girl if that VD tastes anything as tasty as their Spam, I'm sure I will manage to make a beautiful meal out of it!"

How naive, or should I say innocent, at her age too quite oblivious to a seedier side of life. How different to today's generations who are taught sex education almost from stepping in to nursery school. The facts of life as to were babies really appear from, not as we were informed, various ones to choose from, under a rose bush, dropped by the stork, under a cabbage. Looking back I'd have to agree that the truth can harmlessly be cloaked by a little white lie, ignorance certainly was bliss back in those genteel days of old.

WASHHOUSE MEMORIES

As we now revel in our new crowned status of European City of Culture, we some how tend to look back over the decades, and realize how our great and ancient City has changed from the post war decades. In the late forties it was a familiar sight to witness the Mary Ellen's emerging from the public washhouses through out the city garbed in a woollen shawl, a long serge skirt, and a sturdy pair of leather boots.

How deftly they walked with an enormous bundle of freshly laundered clothes. Balanced on top of their heads, a number of these women were paid washerwoman earning not quite a living wage, but in those hard up days of poverty every penny helped to feed and clothe extraordinary large families. In those days eight to ten children was the norm.

Our communities have long since lost the comfort of closeness we once enjoyed, when living in the tenements it gave you the added security of a wonderful close knit family community which consisted of local shops, cinemas, the washhouse, swimming baths, the wash all over's all added to our once vibrant and active neighbourhoods.

The local washhouses were a boon to the local housewives who hardly had the facilities to enable them to wash at home. I loved accompanying my lovely Mam to our local Clare Street washhouse; I attended the crèche for two hours while my Mam completed the family weekly wash. As you walked into the reception area the tiled walls which I can vividly recall. Bright blue painted wooden benches surrounded the white ceramic tiled walls. My Mam being a regular had the privilege of having the use of the same machine and washing stall each week. If you were not a regular you had the inconvenience of having to queue 'on spec' and hope a regular failed to turn up. Who's last on 'Spec' the question constantly being asked as another customer joined an ever-increasing queue.

Two hours of sheer hard graft commenced as the ladies occupied their familiar washing stalls. Working against the clock they were almost likened to well programmed robots. Swiftly filling the troughs with hot and cold water, the washing expertly sorted in to their individual piles. The heavier garments are loaded into the enormous automatic machines. While that task was completed, the back boiler is now ready to accept the special white wash that consisted of white shirts, towels and sheets boiling in a mixture of Reckitts dolly blue, and bleach. The dirtier wash, overalls and jeans followed by the special delicate hand wool wash. Yet again keeping one eye on the clock, while quickly transferring the dripping wet clothes into the huge spinning machine.

After the cycle was completed the clothes were ready for the drying maidens. You had to literally drag forcefully the maidens from the wall the heat escaping was fierce [well most of the time]. The women worked in tandem each helping one another, the camaraderie superb.

The main tasks completed, its now time for a welcomed cup of tea accompanied by the chunkiest piece of golden toast [almost as big as a doorstep] That first sip of tea tasted like the sweetest of nectar, the women sitting at ease in one another's company. Garbed in their washhouse attire turban, rubber apron and a pair of wellies completed the ensemble! The conversation flowed fast and furious discussing every topic under the sun. Births, marriages and deaths were always high on the agenda. Outbursts of raucous healthy laughter echo around the hot steaming walls of the washhouse. The permeating smells of the washing powder accompanied by the strong aroma of the bleach were truly overpowering.

After a deserved ten minute break the women return to their tasks to complete their family wash. Pulling out once again the drying maidens, they begin to quickly strip the now dry and fresh smelling clothes. The final procedure now in sight, the washing stacked neatly in orderly piles awaiting the ironing. Once again they work in pairs, one feeding the garments in to the collander, the rollers roll accepting the clothes. Out they pop on the other side perfectly pressed; my Dads John Ells (underwear) had a perfect crease down each leg! Another week's wash completed in two hours, happily working amongst friends and neighbours, catching up and sharing a little jangle [local gossip]. All part of the wash house culture now logged as part of the City's proud heritage. Safely stored in the archives, yet I am sure they will always evoke extra special memories, again a constant reminder of the gentler times we once lived in. [*Whose last on spec queen*]

The Burroughs Gardens wash house

EVEN MORE WASHDAY MEMORIES

Tuesday was the allotted washday at 33b Fontenoy Gardens. My Mam had an early morning cleaning job in the city centre. Ever pushed for time she had her laundry waiting in the lobby, how industrious they were before leaving the flat, the oven was set on a low temperature, to cook a large casserole, while she completed her weekly family wash. This was a familiar procedure in most of our flats, how organized our Mams were in those days. Talk about having to have a letter from the Holy Ghost to secure a machine in the local washhouse, the washhouse opened half day on a Saturday morning for the convenience of workers who worked full time during the week. In order to secure a washing machine for the chosen few a letter had to be produced from the employer stating that the employee was elegible for a Saturday slot as she worked a five day a week in full time employment.

In our kitchen we had a pulley maiden suspended from the ceiling, on returning from the washhouse, my Mam headed straight into the kitchen. The aroma escaping from the oven was divine, a quick check on the slow cooking casserole, before lowering the maiden, which was my job. I'd pass the damp garments to my Mam who in turn would neatly fill the whole of the maiden. Once full it was hoisted up to the ceiling. The remainder of the laundry was dispersed into each of our allotted drawers in the chest of drawers in the bedrooms.

A visit to the washie was never looked on as a dreaded chore, quite the opposite in fact. You looked forward to the day in order to meet different friends from various districts around the inner city. These friends were your washie mates, which over the years they had became more than just good friends more like confidants. Friendships building stronger over regular meetings, while standing either side of a water trough scrubbing collars and cuffs. Discussing one another's family life.

Once just acquaintances eventually become bosom pals, each inviting the other to join in their family party celebrations. When the washhouses eventually began to close one after the other it was akin to losing a loved one. As the new automatic washing machines and dryers had not quite hit the Manweb showrooms yet, the reliable twin tubs were becoming the vogue, yet still out of the reach of many, as they were quite expensive. The kitchens in the terraced houses were minute as was the tenement kitchens, tackling a family wash for six to eight people was quite an arduous task. The washhouse was really a boon to the working class communities through out the city.

Watching a local wedding while the bride and groom pose for photographs outside the parish church; a spoilsport in the crowd would cruelly shatter the romantic moment forever by shouting to the bride. Make the most of it queen you will be scrubbing his overalls next week at the washie! What a downer on supposedly the happiest day of your life! Yet so bloody true the bride probably would be alongside side her Mam, and relatives who'd guide her through her first wash at the local washie. Once shown the procedure you were out there fending for yourself with a little help from your friends. Though afterwards you were quite chuffed with one's self for completing your first married wash without any mishaps, quite an achievement.

Those happy days seem so long ago, yet loved and sorely missed by so many I bet. Especially at holiday times when the whole flat was practically stripped bare, windows, bed and cushion covers. What a delight to see your washing piled high beautifully washed and ironed. The next generation of washhouse users did not carry their washing on their heads, as did their mothers and grandmothers before them. Instead they made use of their sibling's pushchairs to transport their family wash home. How times changed over the decades in washhouse culture, only the transport part though!

There are so many memories of washhouse days; especially the paid washerwomen who spent most of the day scrubbing other people's dirty washing. One such person was Annie Fitzpatrick a well-known and much respected woman of the Burlington Street community. Her Grandson Pat Reynolds fondly remembers helping his beloved Nin to carry the heavy loads of clothes up the stairs of the tenements. He'd lovingly help her take off her rubber boots. Her poor feet were cold and wrinkled like pig's tripe so tired and aching after almost eight hours on her feet.

Pat filled a large bowl of warm water adding a handful of Epsom salts; his Nin sat for a well-deserved rest while soaking her aching feet. Afterwards Pat sat on a small wooden stool, in order to dry and massage his Nin's weary feet. Annie loved this welcomed treat administered by her favoured Grandson. Pat was truly the apple of his Nin's eye how strong and resilient were those generation of women.

Sometimes if there were a few bob to spare she would take her precious Grandson to the local Gem cinema, both Grandson and grandmother thought each other a precious gem!

Annie Fitzpatrick was quite a character she bore nineteen children including two sets of twins. Annie was renowned as a good hearted woman and neighbour who loved children and regularly helped feed her neighbours when they were most in need of her generous nature and hospitality. Annie was a paid washerwoman for many years she became quite a celebrity when she was interviewed for a topical BBC radio programme. The first interview was conducted by the respected late famous Richard Dimbleby, he was intrigued by Annie's life and somewhat moved by Annie's cheery outlook on life, her humility in thanking God for her good health in order to earn her living and provide for her siblings. How true of the parable *'The meek shall inherit the earth'*. Annie became quite the local celebrity of the district after her earthy interview on life in the inner city for the prestigious world. Annie was once again interviewed for the BBC many years later.

Her other grandson Frank Hennessey recalls yet another famous and popular celeb who later interviewed his Nin for a similar programme, he went on to be the BBCs greatest football commentator and I think will be remembered most for the now famous 1966 world cup victory against Germany with those chosen words.

'There are some people on the pitch; they think it's all over. It is now' shouts the memorable excited tones of the one and only Mr Kenneth Wolstenholme, truly the greatest football commentator of all time.

He too had the pleasure of Annie's wonderful and interesting conversations, thoroughly enjoying the company of a truly remarkable lady, Annie the humble washerwoman who became a celebrity not only amongst her family and neighbours after revealing her wonderful down to earth stories but with her interviewers who were the BBC's 'jewel in the crown' reporters. Annie managed to greatly humble and reduce the might of the famous names to tears associated and revered still at the prestigious BBC! As is Annie, she is still the talk of the parish in the best possible way!

Annie was a paid washer woman and quite a celebrity as she was interviewed for the BBC and left a lasting impression on the famous reporters who had the pleasure of her company and share her personal memories.

Those harsh days can now supposedly be looked on through the preverbal rose tinted spectacles, yet we choose to remember what we cherished in shared relationships with caring neighbours willingly sharing both ups and downs, providing guidance and help when most needed. Values and integrity were the order of the day, respect shown to the older generations, who in those days were held in the highest esteem. Their laden shopping bags willingly carried to their doors by young lads or girls playing in the tenement areas. Sadly times have changed and certainly not for the better, there I go again peering down my fading rose tinted glasses. With a swift wipe I restore the faded lens once again to enjoy the wonderful years we shared in the places we choose to remember so dear to our hearts.

The ironing machine what a boon!

It's all go at the wash house quick march ladies.
'Who's last on spec Queen?'

CHAPTER EIGHT

HER NAME WAS MARY

We were off to Miami to visit our daughter Lisa. It was the summer of 1989. She was presently living there in the very posh district of Coral Gables. Lisa was employed as a nanny to two adorable little girls, Rebecca and Abby.

It was just over six months since we had last seen her. Miami was every thing I imagined it to be. I recall a fragrance of pure refined perfume wafting through the open window of the taxi. The friendly Cuban born driver informed us it was the sweet pleasant aroma of the flowers bougainvillea; it was if the whole area of Coal Gables had just that very moment been sprayed with exotic expensive perfume, it was absolutely gorgeous.

We finally arrived safely outside the beautiful home of the Boswells, tucked away in a corner of the garden stood a very quaint little cottage type building this was Lisa's abode. After all the hugs and kisses it was introduction time. Barbara and Phil were two of Miami's top psychologists. Their oldest girl Rebecca had an uncannily likeness to my daughter Lisa especially her black unruly curly hair. Together we howled with laughter when she pushily introduced herself, she sounded more Liverpudlian than a little yank. Settling in we sat down in the dining room sipping a welcomed cold beer.

It was catching up time; Lisa had three of her friends staying Julie, Joanne and Kelli who were also from Liverpool, luckily Lisa had managed to find them jobs as nannies. It was a case of scousers rule O.K! The girls were thoroughly enjoying their new lives. How lucky these Yankee kids were to have scouse nannies, caring for them, loving them as if they were their own. When the other kids visited with their nannies to Lisa's it was truly hilarious to listen how the Yankee kids now spoke, their accents were now just pure Scottie Road!

Lisa had planned a surprise cruise to the Bahamas, what a fabulous surprise; here we were lazing on the sunny deck of the cruise ship sipping cocktails as you do. When we finally docked at the Bahamas, it was just miles of sun, sand and yet more sand. A white limousine waited for us whisking us away to our hotel, it was situated on the beach. Right this way please Mr and Mrs Donnelly, shouted the chauffeur, a grin on his face the size of the Mersey tunnel. The hotel stood in the middle of the beach, at the rear of the hotel yachts and smaller crafts of different size and shapes were moored.

The palm trees lazily swaying in the balmy breeze, the roasting hot sand running through my toes felt like silk. I was thinking it's a tad different from Moreton beach.

We settled ourselves down near the beach bar, choosing a table, which had an enormous sun brolly as by now the sun, was at its hottest. I was slowly acquiring a nice honey coloured tan of which I was dead proud of. My husband Tommy already had a deep tan. So we didn't look too out of place amongst the other guests who absolutely looked as if they had been here forever. A waiter promptly appeared at our table, hi guys what's your poison asked the lively waiter. Two bottles of Bud please mate replied Tommy. Hey what part of Ireland do you guys hail from asked the waiter whose name we had discovered was Scott. We're from the Capital mate said Tommy, Wow Dublin City hey declares Scott, No Scotty me old mate says Tommy, Liverpool we both chorused together. Revealing that information did it for Scott he became animated shouting excitedly to his fellow waiters. Listen up you guys we have people here from Liverpool, the home of the best group of musicians in the world! Wow had the Donnelly's landed we were now celebrities in our own right.

Further up away from the drinks bar were large areas were food was currently being served, the tantalizing aromas was wafting right across to where we were sitting. Hot dogs sizzling on the hot grills, Scott informed us that these particular hot dogs were renowned to be the most delicious in the whole of the Bahamas, the very best, we were ever going to taste. That particular day you had to queue as there was no table service available for food. We tossed up as you do, I lost, so I joined the orderly line that had now formed. I discovered that the Americans were big on orderly queues, (Unlike us scousers who always managed to find the front of the queue before ever having joined the back of one.) I shouted over to Tommy asking do you want two, I knew what the answer would be, silly question really. Directly behind me stood an American gentleman, I felt a tap on my shoulder, Excuse me Ma'am he said quietly, but with that beautiful accent you surely must hail from Liverpool. Wow the stick our accent has taken over the decades, here I was in paradise being told our accents are beautiful! Have you ever visited our City of Liverpool I enquired? He held his hand out to me, I shook his hand warmly and firmly as you do, remembering one of my Dads pet hates, my Dad hated to shake hands with a person who was false. He always maintained he could judge a person by his handshake. Chuck introduced himself and declared once again that my scouse accent was pure heavenly music to his ears.

How about that, I was about to find out why, he loved our beautiful Liverpool accent, so much.

Chuck readily informed me that he had been stationed at an American air base in Burtonwood, Warrington during the Second World War. On a day trip to Liverpool accompanied by a few buddies from camp, they met up with a few girls. It was when he slipped out for a box of matches to the kiosk he first met a beautiful girl who's name was Mary, Chuck had fallen head over heels with Mary as soon as he clapped eyes on this sweet girl who hailed from Liverpool. I noticed that his eyes were now moist and a look of pure nostalgia spread slowly across his face. His pale blue eyes literally lit up his tanned handsome face, when he spoke her name so passionately. I felt so sad looking at Chuck he was now clearly distressed. He cleared his throat his voice now becoming a little stronger. Continuing with his intriguing story I listened intently as his voice started to falter once again on mentioning Mary's name.

Mary stole my heart and I've had to learn to survive without her, all these years he sighed. Oh my God I could feel my eyes beginning to fill up and my heart was starting to race wildly. I instantly thought of Clarke Gable's parting line from that famous movie 'Gone with The Wind', of 'frankly my dear I don't give a damn'. This was so powerful and memorable even to the present day, quite an unforgettable one-liner in the history of movies. Wasn't It? Until now, I think Chuck is well and truly up there with the better of the famous one-liners. I have never heard anything quite so romantic in all of my life; trust a scouse bird to inflict so much sadness in the heart of one man. Here I was in the Bahamas listening to a still broken-hearted Yank nearly fifty years down the line.

I only wanted a couple hot dogs for Gods sake!! I was well and truly hooked now, forget the hot dogs, maybe I knew of this girl Mary. Chuck continued his story.

He and Mary had met when ever possible. Mary at the time was a qualified staff nurse ministering at the local hospitals in and around the City of Liverpool, Chuck had always met Mary in town; and frequently outside the Northern hospital, which was not very far from my old neighbourhood. When I relayed this information he was clearly delighted.

He was recalling that the hospital was not far from the River Mersey. I confirmed it. He whispered that's the one honey, his voice quite husky now with emotion. A loud voice interrupted our conversation, Please bear with me were having unforeseen problems with the grills, again the voice pleads to be patient; another grill was on its way via the hotel kitchen. Who cares, Chuck continued reminiscing of how he and Mary the girl from Liverpool spent every spare moment together. I inquired being of a typical nosey nature, exactly where did Mary live, he explained that it was not far from the City centre, he remembered Lime Street, were he got on and off the train. Dale Street, that's were they regularly met. Describing the accommodation as a tenement type of dwelling, lots crowded together in a type of square formation.

There were lots of similar type tenement blocks of flats spread all over the inner City so it could have been at least four or five that I knew of, each of them fitting the description mostly all now demolished. Each time he had visited there had been heavy air raids, and everywhere was blacked out. Chuck lifted his Ray Ban sunglasses sitting on to the top of his head; he had the most piercing blue eyes. The tears were now flowing freely down his lean tanned cheeks; He shook his handkerchief out of their neatly folded creases, to wipe his tears away.

I felt so sorry for him on impulse, hugging him, and I whispered are you all right Chuck lad? This simple inquiry brought even more tears. He whispered quite huskily Mary always and ever addressed me as lad; how I loved that special term of endearment. I could feel the biggest lump rising in my throat, I felt like howling out publicly for this lovely former American Officer. I'm quite certain he was a true gentleman.

After the war was finally over he returned to Liverpool trying his utmost to trace his beloved Mary. He had made intensive inquiries all to no avail. He recalls that Mary always stated lets live for today and not make any plans for the future, let's not tempt fate. They were both living and working in dangerous times. He sighed very quietly saying we didn't either. I don't know why I wasn't by now blubbering all over the show, I could only think, this is just one hell of a love story and it involves a girl from my hometown.

The queue was again at a stand still, the girl serving the hot dogs, was apologizing once more for running out of rolls. Who cares, no problem, I was still in a trance listening to Chuck, the Officer and the Gentleman. Chuck had hired the services of a private investigator, on returning to America after the war without ever having any kind of success.

As we talked a very attractive mature woman approached us, wearing a wide brimmed straw hat, which helped to shade most of her face. A colourful sarong covered her ample suntanned body. Her long manicured nails painted a vivid blood red. Her hands were lovely; she wore large diamond rings on each hand. Hi Chuck honey she drawled, what's the hold up? She asked turning towards me, remarking I see you two have become quite good buddies waiting for your hot dogs. She stroked my arm commenting on how fair skinned I was and passing comment that I surely must be an English rose. What part of London are you from? she asked. Just outside I answered taken unexpectedly off my guard, looking straight at Chuck who seemed somewhat relieved by my reply; it was only a little white lie all in the name of love! Wasn't it? I'm Carrie, Chuck's wife, extending her hand to issue a very limp and half-hearted handshake, my Dad, would not have thought much of that handshake. She sauntered off, informing Chuck she was returning on board. Their boat was moored further down from the hotel.

At last the queue was moving at a steady pace, it was my turn to be served, at long last.

Three hot dogs please two with mustard, one with tomato ketchup. Wow speak slowly Ma'am insisted the assistant; I didn't catch one word she drawled. Chuck intervened and rattled the order off no probs. Winking at me with those piercing blue eyes; he also picked up the tab. My pleasure Margaret he said. As I carried the plate of hot dogs to our table, I was well and truly famished by this time. They smelt absolutely delicious, my mouth was literally watering.

I couldn't wait to tell Tommy all about Chuck and Liverpool Mary. Tommy was on his third bottle of Budweiser, stating you can talk for England girl and no kidding. Your wrong I said I've been doing all the listening, honest to God. That must be a first then girl he said, biting in to his long awaited hot dogs smothered with mustard relish, not as good as our mustard though girl says Tommy, licking his chops. Wiping my mouth with my hanky, after the most appetizing hot dog I have ever eaten. I began the saga. Tommy signalled to our new buddy Scott for two more buds, as there was an intriguing tale to be told. And what a tale, could even be a best seller.

Chuck waved and started to walk up from the beach, we waved back turning our chairs towards the beach, I wiped the table down with the unused napkin.

I felt a tap on my shoulder, as I turned around to see who it was, I realized it was Chuck, he kept his hand on my shoulder bending down he whispered in my ear. Would you make an old man very happy and make my heart sing again, for just one more time. In your beautiful Liverpool accent and whisper to me as Mary did so many times as she left me. *tarrah lad!* I felt the tears well up into my eyes. My heart truly ached for this lovely American gentleman. In my beautiful scouse accent I whispered Tarrah Lad, looking through my tears I noticed Chuck's eyes were closed he kissed my hand without looking at me. He then shook Tommy's hand warmly, walking away he didn't look back, he put his hand up in the air walking in the direction to his boat. Carrie his wife was on the deck waiting for him.

During the remainder of the holiday we tried various endings to Chuck and Mary's story. Arriving back at Miami we related our story to Barbara and Phil, wow what a movie that would make. Barbara and

Phil both being psychologists put their slant on the story. Discussing a few theories' maybe Mary was a married woman; her husband maybe at war, there was many other scenarios discussed over the following weeks.

Chuck had checked every possible angle; the investigator came up with zilch. Mary it seemed had vanished off the face of the earth.

In the district of Vauxhall where Mary had often worked in Liverpool, that particular area had the most horrendous bombings, known as the May blitz, the might of the Luftwaffe's air raids had almost totally wiped out a whole community. The fatalities were so high that it was deliberately kept back from the media. On strict orders from our war time Prime Minister Winston Churchill. As the horror of the direct hit unfolded the news was to read even worse, whole families had been wiped out. There were similar reports from around the country but none as devastating as the loss of lives in Liverpool. The moral of the people was at it's lowest ebb. It was deemed that this horror story be kept secret of that terrible night when the inner city of Liverpool was almost totally obliterated off the face of the earth.

After the war ended an open air mass was celebrated in Blackstock Gardens it was attended by hundreds of people in memory of all those unfortunate victims who had lost their lives on that horrific night in May. The citizens of the town centre knew only too well of the night that was never supposed to have happened. Only a few years ago the former neighbours of that devastated district raised enough money to erect a monument to their forgotten memory. Many names appear on the plaque, but many of the poor souls who were killed, their bodies were never recovered. It was reported afterwards in the local press, that only various body parts were discovered, they had literally been blown to bits, how sad.

It was while attending the blessing service of the monument I remembered Chuck's girlfriend Mary she had not showed up for work on that fateful night, maybe Mary too had been one of those unfortunate victims who's remains had never been recovered. I literally shivered and silently prayed for Chuck's girlfriend Mary whom he'd never forgotten or stopped loving after all those years. Love certainly is a splendid thing. This impressive monument now stands proudly in the Vauxhall Road area just a stones throw away from the Northern Hospital where Mary worked in times of emergencies. Chuck informed me Mary was a specialist nurse and was always in great demand from many hospitals, not just in Liverpool. Sometimes she travelled down to the capital if her special nursing skills were required. It was when Father Sibbert was speaking about the cruel losses of generations of families wiped out by evil. Men returning home from war to find not just their homes destroyed, but their precious loved ones lost forever without a proper resting place, how heartbreaking that must have been to accept.

How did they ever manage to cope with such heartache? I recited yet another prayer for Mary, just in case. Maybe that was the reason Chuck had never been able to trace Mary, his ongoing enquiries had always drawn a blank, Mary had not turned up for work that night and as all reports were covered up at that particular time. It was sheer absolute mayhem, the hospital and their workers were run ragged as they had to deal with casualties, evacuate wards which had been badly damaged through the blasts of the bombs falling around the area. At the time none of the harassed staff giving a second thought about paperwork.

Trying to trace missing persons after the war must have been quite a daunting task. Chuck never ever gave up on finding his Mary, for many years after the war he still kept up his own private mission. Sadly he never was to see or hear from Mary again. It was evident on that hot sunny day in the Bahamas one thing was certain Chuck the American pilot had never ever stopped loving his Mary the girl from Liverpool who captured Chuck's heart, not stolen it all those years ago.

Tarrah Mary girl, wherever you may be.

Saint Bridget's procession; the strewing of the petals before the impressive war monument erected in memory of the forgotten war victims of Blackstock Gardens.
May they rest in peace.

CHAPTER NINE

The GIs

My sister Mary and her best friends from our landing in the tenements of Fontenoy Gardens were ever so close, always together carrying their younger sisters and brothers in their mother's shawls. Their hard working mothers cleaning the many prestigious office buildings in the heart of the City.

The girls, to pass away an hour and help to pacify their charges, would take a walk across the Mersey Tunnel entrance to the public park of St Johns. We locals always referred to these beautiful kept gardens as Daddy Bunchies gardens. I don't really know why? Maybe he was the park attendant years ago, that's sheer supposition on my part. I think that may be a question for Frank Carlyle (our local historian).

Daddy Bunchies gardens were a popular haunt for courting couples. My sister Mary and her friends, Teresa Williams and Marie Jones, along with their charges snuggled up so cosy and content in their crochet shawls oblivious to the world. The girls loved to walk around the park gazing at the American service men (who were still over here after the war) with their girlfriends smooching on the park benches. How smart they were in their resplendent uniforms, all loved up. Until the babies started to cry, the girl friends of the 'Yanks' really did not appreciate the din now being created by the kids of Holy Cross. The girls cheekily inquiring 'Any gum chum' to which the girl friends by now were well and truly livid by the intrusion on their privacy.

The officers always asked for a peep at the babies wrapped ever so secure in the snug knitted shawls. They were immediately smitten, and generously gave them a handful of gum, being of a really generous nature they also parted with a couple of shillings, with a parting request to go and buy the kids a pacifier each pronto from the nearest shop!

John's Gardens was the meeting place for the girls and their American boyfriends.

Teresa, Mary, and Marie, delighted with their kindly offerings was now able to drop in to Gianelli's chippie, for a portion of Frank's delicious chips and fish.

A few times a week the girls visited the park, not always as successful as that particular night. Some of the girls in the park with their Yankee boyfriends chased the girls accusing them of being too bloody hard faced and instruct their boyfriends to part with sod all. The girls loved the banter giggling all the way home mimicking the irate girlfriends. Together they talked and dreamed of marrying an American, hopefully being whisked away to live in The United States of America. They could hardly wait to grow up and fulfil their hopes and dreams and eventually meet the all 'American Boy'. Just like ones who visited Daddy Bunchies Gardens.

Dreams sometimes do become reality. Many years later when they had become working girlstarted work; they took the train to

Burtonwood, an American air base situated in Warrington. It was here at this base that two of the girls met their future husbands. Teresa Williams and her next-door neighbour Teresa Williams, both sharing the same surname to distinguish one from the other; one was given the nickname of Willo, a shortened version of her surname.

Mary McKay as I recall was one of the first of many girls in our parish to meet and eventually marry an American. I was only very young but still remember Mary's leaving party, it was attended by her family, friends and neighbours every body so very lively and upbeat until the moment sank in, that shortly Mary was off to live on the other side of the world. The mood changed the songs just got sadder and even more maudlin.

The dreaded time had finally arrived for Mary to take her leave from her adored family and friends. Most of the neighbours had congregated at the end of the landing, which we called the 'Ally O' it was a large balcony at the top of the staircase. With scarves and hankies waving, the neighbours gave a heartrending version of one of Vera Lynn's classics, 'Now is the Hour'. It was that one fateful line in the song which began 'Soon you'll be sailing far across the sea'. That was the cue when the deluge of tears began to flow. Her older brother Douggie practically carried his sister down the stairs in to the waiting taxi. As the singing grew louder Mary continued to bravely wave. There was not a dry eye amongst the neighbours crowded together in the 'Ally O' waving bon voyage. Mary was

Mary McKay in the ATS.

indeed a gorgeous girl we prayed and hoped she'd make a success of her new life in the States. There were many comforting words expressed to her broken-hearted family, who were in fact already counting the days for her first visit home. God love her she had not left the square yet! Mary reluctantly waved goodbye to Liverpool, to begin her new married life in Summit Hill, Pennsylvania, U.S.A.

Her devoted husband Jim was counting the days for her arrival. Mary had served with the ATS during the Second World War, after obtaining her American Citizenship; Mary was destined for bigger and better things. Mary later became the President of her town branch of the American Legion. Another Holy Cross girl to make history in the land of opportunity!

ARRIVAL OF THE YANKEE BOYFRIENDS

The girls from Fontenoy Gardens decided to visit Burtonwood for a big band night, which was being held at the American base near Warrington. It was the very night *the girls were to meet their future husbands.*

My sister Mary and her two friends [The two Teresa's] Williams and Willo each had received complimentary tickets from their firms, in the name of goodwill and friendship to welcome the Americans to our shores. Off they went to Burtonwood arriving by train to dance the night away, to the popular strains of a Glen Miller sounding orchestra. The girls loved every minute, especially as they were the centre of attraction. As usual they were dressed in the height of fashion.

The girls had each caught the eyes of the American servicemen, each securing dates for the coming Friday. At the time they were reluctant to divulge to their parents they were about to date the GI'S. As there was always a suspicion that these young men were over here to have a good time, and their intentions not always honourable. For quite a few months the dates were kept top secret from their parents.

Teresa William's young man Al was a really nice chap he soon became popular amongst the neighbours on B landing. In fact Al quickly became well, almost an adopted son. He was a very handy man especially in cases of emergencies he was such an obliging young man too.

Teresa and Al were later married at our makeshift church in Fontenoy Street. It was such a glamorous wedding; the kids of Fontenoy Gardens were delighted, as Al's buddies from the base attended the wedding. There was plenty of candy being distributed; Al's mates were really good-natured especially to the kids. The wedding reception was held in the Williams family flat at Fontenoy Gardens, as the flat was quite small the furniture was removed with the exceptions of the radiogram and the piano.

Oh what a night the yanks had their first taste of Liverpool's culinary delights. How they loved and enjoyed the deliciously cooked bacon ribs, pig's tails, they were mesmerized, they couldn't eat enough. Next on the menu was the homemade pea soup (pea wack).

The American lads loved the attention they were receiving from the neighbours, milking the sympathy of how they were so far from home. The piano was well and truly tuned, the lads standing around together enjoying a rousing sing a long.

Al and Teresa's wedding was a great success. The American lads loved the people of Holy Cross praising them constantly for their wonderful hospitality. It was always a wrench when the time eventually arrived for the girls to leave to begin a new life on the other side of the world.

Teresa and Al were happily married for over twenty years raising five children together. Later Al was tragically killed in a car accident. When the telegram arrived at Fontenoy Gardens informing his in laws, the news was devastating. The sadness amongst the neighbours, who after a time had begun to look upon on Al, has one of their own. They were truly shocked by his premature death, remembering him as a caring and loving lad. Who together had shared so many happy occasions felt they too had lost a son. Al was just 42 years of age when his life was cruelly taken away; Teresa was totally devastated as was his friends and neighbours of his adopted parish of Holy Cross in the heart of Liverpool.

My sister Mary's guy was named Eddie. Eddie was well over six foot four. Eddie as I remember was really good looking, eventually her closet secret was revealed, at last but very reluctantly in deed, it was agreed the American was to be invited to tea for the 'once over' by both my Mam and Dad. We still laugh to this very day about the palaver Eddie's visit caused. Our flat was given a spring clean, even though the flat was spotlessly cleaned every day by my house-proud Mam. The brasses were polished even more vigorously the windows given an extra polish, they were gleaming. 33B was fit for a visit by the Queen of England

*The wedding party in front of the shelter; looking on from above were the Holy Cross
urchins who no doubt had their issue of American chewy! (Any gum chum?)
(Note the whiter than white washing hanging on the line)*

never mind Eddie the yank. My brothers John and Jimmy and myself
was eagerly awaiting the arrival of 'the yank', I was just five years of
age. Here we were all scrubbed up with our freshly ironed pyjamas.
John was now fed up standing on parade waiting for Eddie he decided
he'd rather be out playing footie with his mates in the square below
our flats. The neighbours too had long given up; they too were fed up
after waiting patiently on the landing for a first glimpse of the
American boyfriend.

My brother Jimmy whispered to me that there was no chance of
Eddie the yank arriving now, so I may as well go to the larder and fetch
him the plate of fresh ham (specially purchased from Gordon's). He
was helping himself to the sandwiches in good style, not as much as a
thought for our VIP visitor. There was also a plate of delicate fresh
cream cakes; they were prettily displayed on a crochet doily on the
cherished family cut glass stand, covered over with greaseproof paper.
Not much of a deterrent for our Jimmy, once the taste buds were
awakened, the fresh cream cakes were next on his agenda.

Eddie was well over an hour late our poor Mary was devastated, she

The Groom accompanied by his American Ushers.
Looks like the girl in the picture is expecting rain clad in her mac and wellies!

kept running up and down the four flights of stairs, (they too had been given a through scrubbing). My Mam and Dad were quite delighted on the sly, seeing there was still not sign of the American boyfriend. One more time she scooted down the stairs, Eddie had finally arrived. He was full of apologies. The train had been cancelled from Warrington, (something's never change) after the excuses were finally out of the way; Eddie produced presents for the entire members of the Gildea family. Eddie's punctuality had well and truly been forgotten. Eddie sat at the table were the best china was making a rare appearance, (having been removed from the glass display cabinet for the occasion) If you could imagine our Mary's face when the sandwiches, minus the greaseproof paper, revealed meatless sandwiches, the culprit made sure he was way out of firing distance. My Mam managed to disguise the cream cakes only just though.

After the food fiasco the ice had truly been broken. Eddie especially had seen the funny side of the situation. It took Mary a tad longer; she threatened to confiscate the American comics and the various candies. Eddie was a very easygoing type; so very generous too, my Dad really looked forward to Eddies visits, as he never came empty-handed. It was his generosity, which immediately won my Dad over, especially the gifts of cigarettes, and a bottle of my Dad's favourite tipple. Not so easy with my Mam she was a different kettle of fish, the Lady was not for turning (so to speak), she never encouraged Eddie to visit, but when he did she reluctantly made him welcome.

Looking back now I think my Mam went along with our Mary secretly praying that the courting lark would sooner or later peter out. It did eventually when Eddie received a promotion, which it meant him being transferred down to the south of England. Absence is supposedly to make the heart grow fonder, not in my sister Marys case. Mary joined by my Dad waved Eddie off on his journey from the platform at Lime Street train station. I would swear that day my dear old Dad was truly gutted, the yank steaming off into the sun, never to be seen again, so much for young love! My Mam's novena had well and truly been granted secretly she was over the moon that Eddie had finally been jibbed. I was broken-hearted my dreams shattered on that Friday afternoon when Eddie left Lime Street station, Eddie not only carried his suitcase from Liverpool, but also all of my hopes and dreams of being a bridesmaid, and spending my six weeks summer holidays riding horses on a ranch, my bubble was well and truly burst on that bright sunny day. I cried for almost a week to help console me my Mam promised me a ride on the donkey's on Moreton shore the coming Sunday afternoon, wow what a compromise!

Thankfully our Holy Cross girls enjoyed their lives in America, making their husbands proud, Liverpool's loss America's gain.

CHAPTER TEN

THE BLESSED HEALING PETALS

Father Tom Williams was delivering his weekly sermon, which at the time he was the serving parish priest at Saint Anthony's, Scotland Road, Liverpool. Father Tom (one of our own) had recently been appointed Bishop of Liverpool.

My family and I attended the ceremony along with many of his parishioners from his former parishes where he had also served. The celebration of his ordination took place at the Metropolitan Cathedral; the lad from Scottie Road has indeed come a long way. How proud we are too of his appointment. It has to be appreciated how much work Father Tom attributed to the church of Saint Anthony's when he took over as parish priest. The crypt below the church is now completed, were there are so many tombs that date back to the early 1800's.

Saint Anthony's church is very special being the mother church in the community the priests at the time were looking after the spiritual needs of the largest influx of Irish immigrants fleeing from their country as the potato crops failed. These dedicated priests literally put their lives on the line attending to the sick Irish who had contacted typhoid. Saint Anthony's is held dearly in the hearts of the inner city parishioner's as being the only church in the district at the time, the priests time was never their own, they were at the beck and call of thousands and they never ever let the poor and destitute people down administering the last rites to the dying, to this present day their kindness and bravery is still remembered.

The Bishop at the time was Archbishop Brown; he had to make a decision quickly about seeking help to alleviate the workload of the clergy of Saint Anthony's. The Bishop contacted the order of the Oblate

Father's who duly obliged, the Oblate Father's arrived in Liverpool from Inchicore, Dublin, at the invitation of the Bishop in order to set up a parish, which later became known as Holy Cross.

Saint Anthony's church stands on one of the most famous roads in the world; the church in fact is almost a shrine to most people in Liverpool. Especially Saturday market day [Greaty] from early hours visitors pop in to light a candle to one of their favourite saints to offer a prayer at one of the beautiful statues at the entrance of the church.

Two of the artefacts are originally from Saint Alban's old church, what a wonderful reminder for their parishioners who can still light a candle and recite a prayer in remembrance of their own cherished parish. Now long gone. Saint Alban's is now a recreation venue with a huge climbing frame that is used regularly to encourage climbing and mountaineering training.

Every Saturday morning Saint Anthony's church is ablaze with glowing candles the heat is fierce on opening the doors. From all over the city visitors choose to light a candle in this magnificent church on Scottie Road were their ancestors once lived before being shipped out to the leafy suburbs to the north and south of the city. A visit to the market also means a visit to Saint Anthony's, an institution all part of our proud Liverpool culture.

Six weeks ago a fire broke out in the church thankfully there wasn't too much damage mostly smoke damage, the cause was stated that one of the bigger candles situated on the main altar had somehow fallen from the holder. Rolling on to the carpet, it beggars belief that the church is still standing with only minimal damage. Bobby Wrigley a saintly man, who diligently and lovingly helped look after the church during the day along with Rita Murphy. Bobby died recently his requiem  was celebrated at Saint Anthony's, Bobby loved and spent every day of the week in the church as he once did in his own beloved parish church of Holy Cross, maybe Bobby had remained on candle duty that day to prevent an even bigger disaster, no miracle, Bobby has not readily relinquished his job, There's no doubt he still keeps a watchful eye on the beautiful church so dear to his heart.

RITA MURPHY

It would indeed be remiss of me if I did not mention Rita Murphy when writing about Saint Anthony's. Rita loved her parish with a devout passion, lovingly cleaning the church since she was fourteen years of age. Rita was on hand to open the church early every morning, going about her work diligently and methodically. Rita was one of the old school brigade she did not suffer fools gladly. Yet she was a kind person, who would listen when she knew another was in desperate need of a sympathetic ear, giving sound advice, which was greatly appreciated by the recipient and believe me there were many.

Saint Anthony's church was so extra special and dear to her heart. When the church closed temporarily after the fire for renovation, I spoke to Rita she was visibly heartbroken, I did not realize at the time she was seriously ill and yet her first priority was still her beloved parish church of Saint Anthony's. When the church eventually reopened Rita was back going about her duties doing the jobs of twenty and that certainly is no exaggeration.

After her unexpected death, we were painfully made aware of just how much work Rita had single-hand undertook and did without any fuss or bother. Rita did it her way the only way the correct way. Father Dunne would be the first to agree, the church almost came to a standstill without Rita's guiding hands, the flowers looked quite sorry for themselves in unattended vases a mortal sin in Rita's book! The money was visibly overflowing from the boxes, candle wax thick on their stands. The once pristine interior and exterior looked in a sad and sorry state in the absence of the 'boss'.

Both Father Grahame and Bishop Tom richly paid homage and rightly so to Rita for her dedication and love that she had unselfishly poured into Saint Anthony's over the decades. Bishop Tom reminded us that when he finally took up the post of parish priest they had quite a few confrontations, the result no clear winner. A mutual respect quickly followed both wanting the best for the best-meaning Saint Anthony's was the overall winner!

Father Grahame requested volunteers in order to help him run the parish it is only fair to point out that he has three other parishes to over see due to the chronic shortages of priests in the archdioceses. His plea was successful, many offered, as there was so many tasks urgently needing attention. Rita Murphy had indeed left a huge void, which sadly and shame on us all who so took for granted the colossal amount of work Rita had overseen for what seemed forever, what ever time of day you popped into church, Rita was present. How true that famous old saying rings *'You don't know what you've got until you lose it'*.

The church once again is back to Rita's high standards after the recent renovations. Yet there is still something missing probably the actual presence of Rita her quirky sense of humour. You are a true legend Rita in the history of your beloved parish were you lovingly toiled, you never ever should be forgotten. It was so fitting that your requiem was celebrated in a packed church each and every one of us giving thanks for your life and services to Gods house.

Rest in Peace, Rita.

Where your name should be revered and marked as a sign of total respect to your memory maybe a plaque inscribed with our thanks for your devotion you were a treasure and should not so easily be forgotten.

Rita Murphy, in the garden
of her beloved church of
Saint Anthony's.

Bobby Wrigley taken before the closure
of Holy Cross Church

Saint Anthony's Union of Catholic Mother's sitting comfortable while enjoying a Christmas tipple judging by the festive headgear!

BISHOP TOM WILLIAMS

Father Tom's opening words of his sermon began;
'Cast your minds back'. Father Tom had a habit of pushing the sleeves of his vestments up his arms while he was preaching.

My eyes were focused on the beautiful array of flowers in the centre of the fabulous main altar; I had noticed that some of the flowers were shedding their petals. They were floating individually, one by one almost in slow motion. Falling on to the cardinal red plush carpet below, the different colours were now scattered haphazardly over the altar carpet like confetti strewn after an extravagant Scottie Road wedding.

I was remembering a glorious summer's day in the month of June 1950, I was six years of age at the time my Dad was sitting in his favourite chair, his newspaper on his lap, his spectacles perched on top of his forehead. He was vigorously rubbing his left eye, my Mam severely reprimanded him once again, and your going to make that eye worse she warned him in a voice she used to us siblings.

My Dad had an awful fear of both doctors and hospitals, since the premature death of his youngest daughter Winifred. He'd already cancelled two earlier hospital appointments. He was finally booked in for an early Monday morning appointment at St Paul's Eye Hospital, Leeds Street. The ingrown warts were now impairing his eyesight inflaming his eye, which was so swollen making it impossible for him to read his Sunday newspapers.

Annie Moran came breezing in to the kitchen, she was my Mam's best friend and neighbour, enquiring how Dads eye was, before he could answer she assured him that with the help of his Blessed and Holy Mother he'd be as right as rain after the operation. Finishing her welcomed cup of tea she mentioned we had all better get a move on. As there was an open-air procession and Benediction taking place that day. Archbishop of Liverpool was the celebrant at our neighbouring parish of Saint Bridget's.

The surrounding Streets of the parish were gaily decorated, paper buntings of red and white, strung across the streets, fluttering swinging to and fro in the warm summer afternoon breeze. The band including the pipes and drums of the Eighth Irish band were in attendance resplendent as ever in their dark green tartan kilts, their leather boots a pristine whiter than white. The pipers so tall and broad shouldered gave them an almost giant type appearance especially to us youngsters. The bagpipes slung across their strong shoulders. The haunting refrains of both pipes and drums playing together literally caused the hairs on the back of one's neck to stand on end. The beautiful young May Queen and her retinue lead the procession, strewing flower petals on to the freshly swept roads.

The Parish priest carries ceremonially aloft the Blessed Sacrament encased in a golden monstrance beneath a gold canopy which had twisted type poles, a bell attached to each corner, securing each side of the canopy. The poles are constantly shaken; it was always a very moving and uplifting moment. As the Blessed Sacrament moved slowly through the crowded streets.

The spectators clamoured in order to retrieve the newly blest petals; fresh and sweet smelling. Lying between the cobblestones later to be carefully collected and taken home for the benefit of sick friends and relations. As over the years they were deemed to have had special healing powers. There was a great but a somewhat friendly rivalry in those wonderful days of pomp and ceremonies of our Noble Roman Catholic Faith, in the surrounding parishes of the Scotland Road area.

Our parish of Holy Cross was up there with the best of them, this year how ever would undoubtedly be St Bridget's turn to be top dog claiming the bragging rights, and rightly so because of the appearance of the Archbishop and his entourage.

I can still recall the most gorgeous smell of the cloying heavy scent of the incense mixing with the light summer fragrance of the various perfume erupting from the flowers, everybody around you dropped instantly to their knees in sheer reverence as the Blessed Sacrament passed.

There was a mad dash to Blackstock Gardens were an open air Benediction was to be celebrated. Our Parish Priest was in attendance when his parishioners spotted him he was given a hearty round of applause, which he duly acknowledged.

The whole of the drab tenements were now transformed with paper buntings in the Papal colours of yellow and white, an altar had been erected to accommodate the impressive ornate monstrance, housing the sacred white host, dozens of lilies adorned each side of the altar, the tenement landings were packed with the residents and their visiting relations. The priests garbed in celebration vestments of gold and rich red material assisted the Archbishop during Benediction.

The Archbishop in his sermon spoke of the tragic events of the Second World War. This particular area was decimated by the constant bombardment dropped by the elite and might of the German Airforce.

The loss of life was so great in the Vauxhall area that it caused Winston Churchill, war time Prime Minister to chose not to divulge or issue any details of the tragedy that occurred during the worst bombing of the entire war on this small close-knit parish of Saint Bridget's nestled in the heart of Liverpool's inner city. This beautiful compact church was later to become another casualty of progress, having to be demolished in order to make way for the building of the second Mersey tunnel. Numerous flats in the parish were also demolished, once again tearing the heart and soul out of that once famous road renowned throughout the world as Scottie Road.

The children strewed the flower petals around the perimeters of the altar area, the Archbishop holding the monstrance high above his head, blessing the crowd. My Mam pushed me urgently forward to gather even more of the blest petals, I carefully gathered them into my hands, carefully transferring; them into the pocket of my pink candy striped dress.

The bands strike up once again the congregation stand for the last hymn in honour of the Blessed Sacrament one of the beautiful old hymns that you rarely hear sung these days. What moving words, 'Sweet Sacrament Divine dear home for every heart'. Sorrowful tears shed openly for the dear departed souls who sadly lost their lives during the Second World War.

St Bridget's processions lead by the CYMS.

The back of our own parish priest (Fr Donavan) the children strewing petals on Limekiln Lane before the arrival of the blessed monstrance.

Benediction celebrated in Blackstock Gardens by the Archbishop of Liverpool
Note the amount of men in their CYMS sashes worn with so much pride.

Returning home I crept quietly into the bedroom, hearing me enter; my Dad called to me, I couldn't help but notice that his infected eye was now almost closed. Sitting beside him I filled him in on the busy events of my day. Carefully tossing the blest and slightly crushed petals on to the bed from the pocket of my dress, the different colours now mixed together looked ever so pretty against the stark plain white starched quilt cover. The over powering fragrances of the flowers filled the bedroom as I sorted the petals carefully one as a time selecting a red one, then an alternative colour of white and violet. My Mam had now joined me at the bedside passing my Dad one blest petal at a time. I heard her whisper softly to my Dad 'Father Son and Holy Ghost, John', as he painfully rubbed his sore infected eye alternatively three times each with the blest petals. His severely infected eye looked even worse, my poor Dad desperately trying to be brave jokingly declared I look as if I've gone the distance with the champion Heavyweight boxer Rocky Marciano! My Mam instructed her husband John to place the blest petals under his pillow which he did so respectfully, the following morning low and behold to our utter amazement the offending warts had vanished.

My Dad winked at me through his lovely now pain free blue eyes, the healing petals have done the trick me girl he gratefully admitted.

I dashed into the bedroom, and slowly lifted the pillow to reveal the petals which had now stuck together in a ball shrivelled up, now void of their gorgeous vibrant colours and fresh fragrances.

My Dad's eyes were now rid of the terrible warts and infection that had blighted his eyesight he had instantly became *the talk of the parish* and the washhouse too for that matter for weeks on end.

CHAPTER ELEVEN

TRADITIONS

Such an old fashioned word describing customs handed down from one generation to another. One religious custom I fondly recall was the wearing of a miraculous medal, especially newborn babies. The medal was secured on to a safety pin which was pinned to the babies vests, transferred daily from one vest to another. When my own two children were born I too carried on this old fashioned Catholic tradition. For the first seven years of your life the medal of Our Lady sat safely on you're under garments in belief that you were kept safe.

Till such times when you received your first Holy Communion then you were on your own minus the hole in your vest! Sadly this lovely old-fashioned Catholic custom has all but faded away, but to be fair to this new generation I have noticed a miraculous medal pinned to the hood of the designer prams. Maybe just the location has been changed for health and safety reasons. I'd like to think so.

Another noble tradition missing from church services are the various confraternity masses. Each confraternity had a particular Sunday reserved in the month first Sunday was allotted to the children of Mary. In those days there was no discrimination it was the done thing ladies before gentlemen!

The ten o'clock mass was always the childrens mass our teachers always in attendance to usher their pupils into the allocated benches in the front of the church. How poignant when the children sang at various times of the mass, you have to remember in those days the mass was celebrated (again that word tradition) in the Latin format. It was quite easy for the younger kids to lose interest it was inevitable that there was always a 'few kick offs' in between hymns. I can honestly say hand on heart how I do prefer the traditional hymns from our school days. Even to the present day when one pops up, usually at funerals, you are immediately fast forwarded back to the bench in your old parish church, not realizing that you're singing top note and word perfect!

The eleven o'clock Mass Second Sunday in the month was celebrated for the C Y M S of the parish, it was quite an impressive sight the men garbed in their Sunday best, suited and booted sporting a navy blue sash. Their obligation to their sodality was to attend mass and Holy Communion once a month. The front benches were allocated for the men each bench had the banner with the initials 'C Y M S HOLY CROSS', embroidered in gold letters. After mass the men congregated outside the church, having a smoke and a chat to the priest to while away the time until the parish club opened.

Then it was time for a pint and a game of darts or billiards. The parish clubs in our communities were a hive of activities as the individual teams were ran and organised from the club.

The men enjoyed the camaraderie which being part of the Catholic Young Men's Society created.

Each parish had their own football teams, billiards and dart teams which they were indeed proud of, meeting up and playing one another each week enabled them to strike up good friendships. Until the game commenced and that was when the friendships ended, on the sports field it was game on, wanting their own proud parish to be victorious, the good name of the parish was at stake, believe me there was no prisoner's taken!

THE CHILDREN OF MARY

The children of Mary were always well attended smartly garbed in their blue cloaks and white net veils. Again the front benches were allocated for them, the same format as the men, they also had their own banners at the end of each pew, which they carried with much pride on the occasions of our prestigious outdoor May processions.

The older members took the younger members under their wings, arranging holidays to Ireland, probably their first holiday in their lives. The Isle of Man and the south of England were other destinations the girls enjoyed. Always heavily chaperoned by the older members to ensure they girls never stepped out of line. The Holy Cross girls misbehave, never! The girls particularly loved their visits to the Emerald Isle, especially the dances that had been arranged beforehand to welcome the glamour girls from Holy Cross.

My sister Mary and her friends Marie Jones and Teresa Williams, how they loved and looked forward to their jaunts with the group. The girls also had a concert group performing musicals, plays and festive pantomimes. I could not wait to grow up and join this glamorous group of girls. After mass they'd mill around the church minus their cloaks, displaying the most fabulous clothes, dressed in the height of fashion. Not just pretty faces either they put on tremendous shows raising funds for the restoration fund.

THE WOMAN'S CONFRATERNITY

My Mam was a member, she wore her medal on a blue silk ribbon over her Sunday best coat. I still have the medal to this day, I take it out occasionally and it never fails to trigger off a series of memories of a once golden era in my life. May processions were the highlight of the parish activities; we were never to forget the occasion was to honour our Blessed Lady. I loved the pomp and ceremony of the outdoor processions, the atmosphere of the crowds who lined the streets.

The different bands in full regalia, added even more to the occasion. No matter how many times you were to witness the ceremony of the crowning of the statue of our Blessed Lady, the scene still moved one to tears, whatever parish you still felt the same emotion as the May Queen placed the crown on the statue. Another time honoured tradition lost and relegated to the vaults of the archives

Holy Cross pensioners in the parish club at their Christmas party celebrations.

*The CYMS in procession; what a turn out? This particular Holy Cross
procession was the largest Catholic gathering on record in 1913.*

*May Queen Marie Conncannon and her retinue taken on the shelter in Fontenoy Gardens in 1957
I am pictured next to Cath Silker, Marie McGowen, Veronica Curran, Patsy Delehunty, Ann
Bernia, Judy Santamera, Kathleen Mullhall, Ellenore Savage, and Mary Devine.
Shelia Redhead (cushion carrier) and Mary Thompson.*

TRADITIONS THAT DO STILL CONTINUE

The one tradition I can think of which has not changed over the decades are the wakes in our inner city communities I can vouch that the wake tradition is still (forgive the pun) alive and kicking! Maybe the occassion is not as intense and sombre as in the past.

The night before the funeral the ritual of family and friends unite to recite the five decades of the rosary, such a comfort to the bereaved relations. Afterwards there's a drink to help unwind and meet once again old friends and neighbours who have come from far and wide, in order to pay their last respects.

Once again to relive the good old days to tread once more down the hallowed pavements of memory lane.

The Requiem mass has thankfully changed to one of celebration in place of a once doleful service, now there is laughter as a family member delivers a personal eulogy, spontaneous applause rings around the church from the congregation. The priest delivers his sermon more of a tribute to the deceased than a sermon relating to the burning fires of purgatory and hell. Another personal touch, a favourite song played in memory of the deceased to help ease the last sadness of their final journey.

The welcomed changes made to the Requiem service has certainly changed for the better. The priests' vestments are now bright instead of the severity of the mourning colours of black and purple.

COACH TRIPS

I'm glad to write that the coach trips tradition in the parish of Holy Cross are still going strong we now travel in coaches instead of charabancs the destinations to Wales to the shrine of Saint Winifred at Phantasph in Holywell, still walking in our ancestor's footsteps so to speak. Blackpool has disappeared from the agenda, we have gone slightly upmarket.

The Lakes, Shakespeare country, and the beautiful York Minster. A tiny bit of culture has crept in to the itinerary over the decades, well, we do have to lead by example to celebrate being crowned 'Capital of Culture'.

TRADITIONAL PAWNBROKER'S

Traditional pawnbroker have well and truly vanished. I remember with so many fond memories Berry's our friendly neighbourhood pawnie. Berry's was located halfway up Richmond Row, not a stone's throw away from our flats. I've heard that most pawnshops were affectionately known as uncles. Suppose our community had to be different ours was in fact Aunt's. Aunt Edie's to be politically correct, she served behind the counter, which was really high. Most of the punters used the back entranceso they wouldn't be seen by the neighbours. I don't know why because almost every one at one time or another had the need to visit Aunt Edie.

Aunt Edie was quite flamboyant; she had bright red hair, enhanced by a bottle of Banners finest Henna. She wore a bright flowered three-quarter overall. I loved to visit the shop with my friend Teresa Conway; she ran an errand for a neighbour a bundle of bedding and an astrakhan coat.

The grateful precipitant rewarded us both with a thrippny-joeys each, mission accomplished. Monday was sheer bedlam the busiest period for Aunt Edie, the same question was continually asked how much are you asking? Aunt was a dab hand at bartering, never giving the asking price always considerably less. After the done deal you were issued with a ticket, you produced the ticket when you returned to redeem your goods. I really did love visiting the popshop, as there was no shame really by an occasional visit as it sometimes kept a roof over many a neighbour's head, ours included. My brothers John and Jimmy hated visiting Aunts, they didn't mind redeeming the goods, as this procedure was much quicker than the first transaction. After Aunt located the bundle she would proceed with the calling of your name. This incident always baffled me, as the women never divulged their married names, they used their maiden names. Saving face if discovered by a neighbour they pretended the transaction was for their Mam!

The back of the shop was really cold and damp, quiet dilapidated in fact. At the front of the premises the area was quite bright. The window had quite an impressive display unit with an array of watches and various kinds of jewellery. Diamond rings, signet rings, plenty of choices if you only had the dosh to splash out, which were very rare in our neck of the woods.

Most of the items of jewellery were unredeemed pledges; this was stated under the price card.

I was delighted when my Mam and Dad purchased a marquisette ring for my fifteenth birth, also for the occassion of my leaving school. I felt so grown up and could not stop looking at my finger supporting a beautiful sparkling diamond ring, well almost diamonds.

Not caring a jot that it was probably one of the countless unredeemed pledges of Aunt Edie's.

I sincerely hope you have enjoyed this nostalgic and leisurely stroll down through the decades as much as I have. Fondly recalling where we were born and bred. A double helping of nostalgia does one's heart and spirit the world of good. Enabling one to digress and count ourselves, oh so lucky to have enjoyed the friendships and most of all the camaraderie of a close knit community.

Living amongst honest and hardworking people in our tenement dwellings were respect, good manners, but most of all family values were utmost on the agenda. Nostalgia can sometimes be bitter sweet if you allow yourself to dwell too long. Instead count your blessings before dropping off to sleep, be grateful that we lived in gentler times, were respect was earned and in return honoured.

Those were the days my friends, indeed so very, very special.

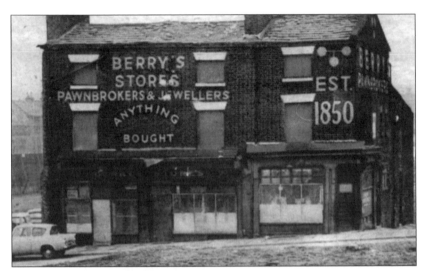

Berry's Pawnshop Richmond Row.

THE BEST DAY OF THE WEEK

When I was a child I always and ever looked forward to Sunday as I always felt it was a special day especially in our tenement flat situated at the bottom of Scottie Road.

33B Fontenoy Gardens sounds very posh, a garden without flowers, never ever bothered me though what you never had you never missed. Sunday always began with a visit to morning mass, returning home to a gorgeous cooked breakfast. Ready prepared on the table was bacon, egg and crunchy golden fried bread. I was absolutely ravenous after having fasted from midnight the previous night. Dipping that golden fried bread into my perfectly fried egg (which in those days the yolk seemed to be as big as a pancake) was such a mouth watering experience. I can still close my eyes and instantly remember that first dip into that pale new laid yolk.

After breakfast it was the same scenario in every other flat on our tenement landing, preparation of the Sunday roast almost a ritual. My older sister Mary always helped with the cleaning, while I was enjoying a game of two balls, with my friend Mary Kennedy in the 'ally-o', which was situated at the end of our landing. Pounding the wall, one a penny two a penny Walls ice cream.

Oh Happy Days.

Looking out along the landing of our tenements most of our older sisters were on their knees scrubbing the step and landing, all in lively conversation about their Saturday night out on the town. The wireless tuned in to the same radio station,

Featuring the ever popular programme of that time, BBC's Two-way Family Favourites. The girls sang along in tune to the popular songs of the fifties.

Two-way family favourites was broadcast every Sunday between 12 o'clock and one, it was a Forces request show, when a lad from 'Fonnie oy' was mentioned the girls were all screaming Its for Billy Gannon he was at the time stationed overseas on his national service, which the lads had to endure in those days, fame at last.

A mention on the BBC. His request was for Johnny Rae singing his latest recording.

After family favourites we had a visit from the clergy this week it was

Father Murphy our parish priest. Sandy Bromilow one of the parishes funniest characters would announce beforehand what priest was visiting. Sandy's voice would wake the dead as well as the banging on the recently polished knocker. Both my sister and brother dashed into the bedroom at the sound of Father Murphy's voice.

Why this was because my brother John was an altar server and recently had been missing without permission from his altar duties. Mary my sister was in hiding because Christmas was fast approaching and Father Murphy expected Mary to sell at least 20 books of raffle tickets, which was her excuse!

Our Clergy seemed to have extraordinary memories because they remembered every persons name in each household they visited as well as remembering the dogs and budgie's names an incredible feat as our parish at one time was one of the largest in the archdioceses. Father Murphy was indeed a larger than life character he just did not know the meaning of the word 'can't' or the word 'no', not in his book or I should say in his bible! As he shook hands with my Dad he inquired 'no sign of the siblings today?'.

My Mam's face was a picture of guilt but Father Murphy gave her a knowing wink. As he walked into the hall he banged on each of the bedroom doors, addressing both of the bunkers in his broadest Irish brogue, Mary I will pass 50 books of raffle tickets next week for all your colleagues at Littlewoods pools. John I will see you at 9 o'clock sharp tomorrow morning we have a requiem mass, Dan Murray has given you permission so there's no probs for you being late for lessons. He had a smile on his face as wide as the river Mersey as he left 33B. Both my parents were doubled up in laughter when John and Mary came sheepishly out of hiding. Mary was absolutely livid at the thought of having to flog 50 bloody books she was not a happy bunny by any means.

John was not too fussed by being rumbled by Father Murphy as he didn't mind assisting at weddings and funerals as afterwards he would be a few bob better off, rubbing his hands together he declared Father Murphy's bark is much worse than his bite once he's given you a verbal rollicking he's sweet till the next time.

My Dad was still chuckling while addressing his two children saying 'there was a good lesson to be learnt there for you both never try to kid a kidder especially when his name is *Father Murphy*'.

One thirty on the dot, our dinner was served, ready and waiting on the table. I'd skip along the landing, passing the back kitchen windows, which were opened wide, wafting gorgeous smells of the different veg cooking. The tantalizing aromas of roast meat were permeating through out the flat as I opened the door. The table laid with a snowy white tablecloth, the table extended to accommodate the six of our family around the table. With the help of my sister Mary my Mam carried in the plates, steaming hot, my favourite meat roast lamb, crispy roast potatoes and an assortment of fresh veg. My two brothers John and Jimmy as usual would engage in their weekly fight about who had the most roasties on their plate. Digging one another and giving each other sly kicks under the table. Both of them moaning about Mary choosing the crispest spuds she'd give them both a playful slap across the lugs.

My Dad prepared a jug full of shandy for us to enjoy with our dinner. For our puddings we had homemade apple pie, the hot apple oozing from the eyelets in the middle of the pie. Hot custard poured over from a tall jug which had lovely hand painted roses on which had once belonged to my Nan. I can almost taste the gorgeous pie light golden pastry with a smattering of sugar across the centre.

Directly after dinner my Dad always and ever made the same statement, "Well that's me off to bed for forty winks after that delicious meal". Forty winks really meant roughly about four hours. No such luxury for my poor Mam it was back in the galley to clear away, and prepare for an afternoon of baking. Rhubarb pies, scones, and apple turnovers. Delicious smells of freshly baked pastries, cooling off on the windowsill on a wire tray. I could never resist poking my finger into the middle of the pie when the filling oozed out, burning the finger off me delicious!

Sunday to me was so special, it was the only day really that we all sat around the table together as a family, during the week we arrived home at different times.

How times have changed, most people now opt out of all the hassle of cooking on a Sunday, not like our dedicated Mams who worked so hard of a Sunday to make it extra special for us to spend together as a family. Sunday was never a day of rest for them. As Josie McGrail my old school friend always reminds us at our parish reunions, that we really were so blest with wonderful Mothers how very true, looking back I realize how we so took them for granted in those days of growing up.

This quirky painting, (Under the Arch) was delightfully painted by Lynn Gallagher Fontenoy Gardens minus the shelter. (There are a few familiar characters depicted can you spot them?)

CHAPTER TWELVE

MEMORIES LAST LONGER THAN DREAMS

What's that scar on your knee nanny, asked my granddaughter Katie, who was seven at the time. I've had that scar since I was your age, I replied, Wont that ever go away, she asked, always the inquisitive one.

Looking down at the still clearly visible scar, I touched it, remembering the night that I acquired it. My class was taking part in an Irish theme night being performed at the parish hall in Fontenoy Street directly next door to our parish Church of Holy Cross. Our beautiful Church was wantonly destroyed by enemy bombers during the Second World War. The premises were to be our temporary home while waiting for our new church to be rebuilt. The tickets had been sold out for weeks; I'd devoutly been reciting Novenas to Saint Anthony to help me be chosen for the dance troupe.

Promising if I was chosen I'd donate my entire pocket money to his collecting box for the poor. I'm sure he wasn't canonized just for his ability in finding lost property. In the past I can honestly admit that Saint Anthony has never let me down yet, especially when asking for a special favour.

I was chosen for the troupe, and elected as leader; I warranted my granted intention was well worth two weeks pocket money. Miss Haynes was our music teacher she was adored by all of her pupils, she possessed such style I adored her. She had the most powerful operatic voice, which sounded so sweet and beautiful.

I couldn't wait to get my little legs up the tenement stairs to inform my Mam and Dad about my great news, as I had them persecuted all week long, asking them constantly. If they thought, I would be chosen to take part in the forth-coming school concert.

I had obtained two tickets now tucked safely in my gymslip pocket.

They were ever so posh white embossed cards printed in gold. My Mam placed them both behind the mantle clock for safe- keeping.

All of the proceeds being raised were going into the restoration fund for the new church.

I couldn't stop looking at the tickets, which read 'A *Night of Entertainment with Special Guests, and Introducing, the Holy Cross Irish Dancing Troupe*'.

I was so excited I couldn't wait for Thursday night; I couldn't sleep a wink. Tuesday afternoon the dancers were summoned to the sewing room for the final fitting of our costumes.

Mrs McCallum along with the older senior girl's help had truly worked like Trojans to have them completed for the big night. Our tops were made of white seersucker material, embroidered with green sparkly sequins; they had tiny tight puff sleeves edged in gold sequins. The skirts were made of black velvet, with a full circular skirt, edged in gold. In the centre of the skirt sat a shamrock of green and gold sequins, they were absolutely gorgeous. I was ecstatic; I really did think I was the bee's knees.

Miss Haynes suggested to the girls with long hair to wear it loose, just for the show. Which in turn delighted us all as our hair was always restricted in two fat plaits. Gazing in the full-length mirror, the sun shinning through the long elongated window, which shone directly behind me, almost like a spotlight I felt I was already on stage. Let the music commence, I couldn't wait for Thursday night to arrive.

I still had not slept a wink for the next two nights, the adrenaline was bubbling inside me, eventually Thursday night arrived, the hall was filled to capacity not an empty seat to be seen Miss Haynes again quickly ran through our routine, once again giving us our last minute instructions. We the dancing troupe were to open the show and close it. Wishing us the best of luck, and while doing that she crossed her fingers "Go and knock them for six, you will be tremendous, just look to Margaret for guidance"

I was as proud as those beautiful peacocks strutting around the park at Otterspool promenade. While Miss Haynes stood in the wings, the music rang out loudly around the smoke filled hall, we took our places and began to dance, our black tipped shoes resounding in tune to the rousing music. The troupe danced perfectly not one practiced step out of our planned routine. The applause rang out spontaneously, leaving the stage to a rapturous ovation.

Mr Dan Murray our Headmaster was waiting backstage to congratulate us. Orange juice was supplied drinks all round, how we needed them we were sweating cobs.

Our make up which had been caked on to our faces was now running down our necks a towel was hurriedly found, which helped to absorb our sweaty little gobs. We were so happy and naturally on a high after such a perfect performance the amount of strenuous rehearsing had paid off. Mr Murray reckoned we were going places and expected us to be in high demand in the near future as we had performed so professionally.

Miss Haynes stepped in expressing that was enough praise for the moment the job still needed to be completed. Reminding us all, that as we the troupe were the last ones on stage we were the ones, who will carry the whole show on their shoulders. At no cost could mistakes be afforded, she knew how to bring us all back down to earth.

We were given instructions to sit quietly and wind down. We listened to the other various artistes entertaining the appreciative audience. The applause rang out around the hall as partaking artistes in turn took their final bows. The singer was crooning away sounding just like the famous American singer Bing Crosby. The crowd was thoroughly enjoying themselves participating in the song, Moonlight Bay, I peeped out to witness my Mam and our neighbours Mrs Kennedy and Mrs Silker enjoying the singers version of the song the audience were having a ball. The curtain fell with Mr Dan Murray announcing a short interval for the sale of refreshments and of course there was to be a raffle. The Children of Mary girls were doing the honours serving tea with Marie biscuits and McDonald's chocolate marshmallows donated by our friendly corner shop Annie Ryan's. The Ryan families were very generous benefactors to the church.

The audience had returned to their seats eagerly awaiting the finale; the lights in the hall are slowly dimmed the coughing subsides; the audience settling down; a hush descends across the packed hall. Miss

Haynes sings in her beautiful soprano voice, you could have heard a pin drop. Her voice so strong, I'm convinced she could be heard as far off as the Pierhead. As she took her applause, she signals to us to be on stand by we were to follow the next act. The crooner had the audience singing along to a medley of Al Johnson hit records of that particular decade, the crowd thoroughly enjoying the participation.

At the end of his performance he was given the traditional Holy Cross send off, 'Nothing could be finer than to be in Carolina in the morning', sang the crowd enthusiastically there were three encores he took his bows graciously it was now our turn once again to entertain our appreciative audience.

The red velvet curtain ever so slowly opened, the music struck up immediately I was the last one to climb up the steep wooden rickety stairs. When suddenly it happened, my knee came in to contact with a sharp rusty nail that was protruding from the wood.

The huge nail ripped right through my skin. I could feel the blood trickling down my leg. My adrenaline was so high, and feeling so proud of myself and thinking how wonderful the troupe had performed I thought the show must go on. I could now hear Miss Haynes voice encouraging us to go out and perform. I danced my way to the centre of the stage, my hair swinging, my feet tapping to the beat of the reel, forgetting the sore bleeding knee. My partners and schoolmates were dancing so beautifully; once again we never put a foot wrong. The audience did us proud clapping, cheering and whistling; they gave us another standing ovation the hall was in uproar with our performance as we took our final bows the curtain fell and so did I. My close mates, Mary Lawrence and Angela McGinn ran to me, trying to pick me up. When Angela saw the blood she screamed for Miss Haynes, Mary Moore my other friend had put her hand over the gash to try to stem the flow of blood. I felt I wanted to be sick, I don't remember being carted off to the Northern Hospital. The gash required five stitches, the scar still clearly visible to this day my Dad rightly predicted that I would be marked for life, but a brave little trouper nonetheless, the show must go on and by golly it did. Memories certainly do last longer than dreams. I know I have the scar to prove it!

CHAPTER THIRTEEN

THE LATE MRS CATERHAN

It was almost a summer's day, more likened to June than late September. The sun shone gloriously as I opened the door which led to a small veranda, part of our comfortable Corporation owned tenement flat. Fontenoy Gardens overlooked the busy Scotland road area. At eight o'clock in the morning the traffic was at its heaviest, another hectic day in progress as the traffic made its way towards the famous Mersey tunnel.

Glancing up at the beautiful clear blue sky, there was not a sign of a cloud. I decided that I'd wear a pretty summer outfit for my trip into town. It's gorgeous out here Dad I shouted over the din of the heavy traffic. My Dad was sitting in his favourite armchair, legs outstretched before him reading his daily morning paper. He worked night shifts for British Railways; he found it hard going in making the change to not working with his beloved horses. My Dad had been a carter for most of his life, loving his every working day relationship with his horse and beloved companion Sandy, my Dad had previously won many awards for the best-turned out horse in the Lord Mayors parades.

Stepping out on to the veranda he bent his head to catch a whiff of the flowers still blooming in the wooden window box, our small veranda was brightly whitewashed, the concrete floor bleached and scrubbed regularly by my house proud Mam.

Stretching up his arms slowly, he sighed rubbing the back of his neck, you're right girl I think were in for a scorcher of a day, make the best of it and get out there Mags, he said as he yawned wearily. I had taken a few days leave from my job at Plesseys, situated in Cheapside

115

off Dale street further up on the opposite side stood the famous Bridewell.

I had to complete a last few arrangements for my forth-coming wedding.

That was taking place in just three week's time. Tommy my husband to be was having his final fitting for his wedding suit. We were also collecting my outfit for the evening reception from Lucinda Byre in Bold Street. I had really splashed out on my outfit for the evening reception; the clothes were fabulous in that era, being the start of the swinging sixties.

It was 1964, the City of Liverpool was really the place to be, especially the music scene. It was such an exciting, place to be and to be a part of. The City always a vibrant place was now almost ready to explode with the many groups who would eventually go on to conquer the world. The football wasn't too bad either. Liverpool F C won the F A cup for the first time in their history in May 1965. The good times were only just beginning for our great City. I was so excited the wedding arrangements where at last finally in place, we were to be married in my parish Church of Holy Cross on the 19th of September at 1 o'clock. Father Cronin had recently moved on to the Channel Islands leaving me broken-hearted. I had received a letter that morning assuring me that he wouldn't miss the day for anything in the world! I was elated so was every parishioner in the parish as he was a very popular priest, there would be plenty of time for him to catch up on all the news and goings on in the parish.

Tommy hadn't really warmed to Father Cronin as he mentioned at his first meeting with him stating that he was really disappointed with Margaret for not choosing a good Holy Cross boy instead of going to another neighbouring parish. Tommy had struck up a good relationship with Father Cronin's successor, Father Sheridan. He was more on Tommy's wavelength. Father Sheridan loved his 'footie' running a very successful Y M C S parish team. I was really becoming nervous as the time was drawing closer, not that I was having cold feet, God no I adored my Tommy he is the love of my life, it was just that we had no place to set up home as yet. Whenever I mentioned this worry, he'd always mimic his Mam and say (Gods good and his Holy blessed mother something will turn up).

With each day I was growing even more anxious, the wedding was now only two weeks away, and still no place to live. There wasn't any room in our flat; the situation was even more acute at Tommy's, in fact, serious overcrowding problems at 48 Portland Gardens. Tommy's sister Vera along with her husband Tommy also their three children, five in all accommodated in just one bedroom. His youngest sister Sheila and his Mam occupied the third bedroom. Tommy's bedroom was so tiny you literally could not swing a cat. The housing problem really was phenomenal in the early sixties with most married couples having to rely on relations to rent them a room until they were able to save for a decent deposit on a terraced house, it was so difficult in them days, as there was an acute shortage of living accommodation, thus the building of high rise flats which proved to be a salvation at the time resolving the shortage if only on a short term basis. The thought of having to start our married life in that tiny room scared me senseless, I had struck up a great relationship with my nearly in laws, but still did not relish joining an already overcrowded abode.

Tommy came breezing into the kitchen, he was so easy going, nothing ever fazed him, he was having a conversation with my Dad over Liverpool's chances in the forthcoming cup competition, my Dad loved teasing Tommy about Liverpool winning that most valued and prestigious trophy, which my Dad had longed to win, along with every other Liverpool fan in the City. He always said (when L F C finally do manage to win the F A cup the Liver Birds will take flight) My Dad slipped Tommy a quid to enjoy a drink on him. Walking hand in hand through town I mentioned how worried I was at still not having any where to live after the wedding, Tommy always the optimist as always said, 'don't be worrying something will turn up you'll see'.

In the early 60's it was the norm to start your married life living with your parents until you qualified to join the council waiting list and that sometimes could take years. I decided to dismiss all my fears and enjoy the day out on the town Our first stop being the bespoke tailors in Dale Street, Tommy was having his final fitting for his three piece suit, he had chosen navy blue mohair, with being so blonde it was a good choice, even covered with big bold white stitches the cut looked sharp. Mr Abraham complimented Tommy on his choice, over the years Tommy and his tailor had struck up a close relationship, once again he'd be an excellent advert for Mr Abraham's of Dale Street. After shaking hands and wishing for us both the best wedding day ever, also assuring us both that Tommy's suit would be ready on time for the big day.

Watson and Prickard in North John Street was our next port of call were Tommy chose his shirt and tie and cufflinks, when my Dad heard how much they'd both cost he declared he'd want a suit and overcoat for that amount of dosh.

That was the bridegroom sorted now for the bride. Off to Bold Street, I loved shopping in this quaint cobbled street it was at one time the most prestigious street to shop in Liverpool. The only time my Mam visited Bold Street was to attend her cleaning job. Our shopping spree over, we walked along taking a short cut through to Seel Street, it was only then that I noticed a Catholic church.

I never knew this quaint church existed. I coaxed Tommy to come in with me and say a little prayer for a special intention. Entering the church I whispered to Tommy, as it was our first visit, we could request a favour (you can take one guess at what mine was). My Mam always believed that wishes could be granted on a first visit to a church you had never visited before, here goes. Please God, please God, our Lady of Lourdes grant me our wish. (Somewhere to live) I prayed like I'd never prayed before, for a place of our very own to start our married life.

The original St. Peters Church.

It was so cool inside this old but beautiful classical church, Tommy knelt in the pew in front of were I was lighting the candle to our Blessed Lady as I placed the candle into the holder I noticed an old lady dressed really old-fashioned, she was dressed from top to toe in black. She wore a small velvet hat perched at the back of her head. Her hair was snowy white, thick waves covering each ear. In her hand was an oily cloth which she was vigorously cleaning the tray below the lighted candles, were the wax had accumulated.

She smiled at me the smile lit the whole of her face up, she looked so ethereal, and kindly so at home in Gods house. I related to her that it was my first visit to St Peter's and asked her would she pray for us both as we had no place to live after the wedding. She kept busy scraping the candle grease from the tray.

I whispered goodbye and waved as we reached the back of the Church, she acknowledged me waving back. For some reason I felt so uplifted and so very content with myself.

Wasn't that old lady lovely Tom? What old lady? asked Tommy. The one I've been talking to for the last five minutes, while I was lighting my candles.

I never seen you talking to anyone, we were the only two in the church.

Oh give me strength I thought, I'm not letting him wind me up so I decided to keep quiet. Today there was to be no skimping, we had saved so hard for our big day, we were now going to treat ourselves good style, splashing out like never before. On entering our favourite Chinese restaurant, Mr Jack Hue welcomed us. Two weeks of freedom left that's all I have Jack, Tommy quipped.

Mr Hue smiled at Tommy's comments, he had a gorgeous smile, he was always so fresh looking, as if someone had just polished his face and bald head. Directing us to a place by the window, Tommy ordered a bottle of **Beaujolais**, we certainly were pushing the boat out!

The waitress poured the wine inviting us to taste, Tommy swirled the wine around in his mouth much to the amusement of Mr Hue, thumbs up, and Tommy proffered his glass for a top up. A compliment to you both from Mr Hue, and his staff.

Nice one Mr Hue, shouts Tommy both of us raising our full glasses. After accepting Mr Hue's good wishes we left the restaurant in really high spirits we were having a lovely day so far.

After lunch we strolled arm in arm through St Johns Gardens, the perfume from the plants and flowers smelt even stronger from the warm balmy breeze. It was such a lovely day for the time of the year; my Dad could well be right with his forecast of an Indian summer. Just in time for a certain wedding that's soon to take place. I felt so light-hearted maybe that was through the effect of the wine, maybe more dizzy than light hearted. Again I thought about the old lady at Saint Peters, that lovely serene smile, dressed so old-fashioned, she reminded me of my own Nan. Wearing a long serge type skirt with about three different types of petticoats underneath, enabling them to flare out almost likened to a crinoline dress.

Did your Ninny Bennett wear clothes like that old lady in church today? I enquired, which old lady are you on about?

Oh Tommy stop winding me up now didn't you see her when I was lighting the candles?

Honestly girl I was watching you lighting the candles so pious. I thought you looked lovely.

Oh shut up, I replied I knew it, you're always the same skitting, now turn it in and tell the truth and shame the devil did you see the old lady?

Honest to God girl, wetting his forefinger he recited like we did when we were kids, reciting criss cross if I dare lie my mother will die.

I knew at that precise moment he was telling me the truth, he had definitely not seen the old lady.

Oh forget it lets go and have another drink before we head home, he was now starting to annoy me. 'I could murder a pint of mild, after all that shopping and walking about its made me quite thirsty', he said.

Arranging my wares around me, Tommy eventually sauntered over from the bar with our drinks. It was at that precise moment when Frank joined us at our table; he was one of Tom's workmates at the docks. With the typical scouse humour Tommy informs Frank that he spotted him hiding under the table waiting till he had been served. There was always the same banter going from one to another, Frank hit back with you know how much I love Margaret I thought you was with the other Judy you knock about with, with that remark Frank plants a big kiss on my cheek. Frank and Tommy were old schoolmates as well as workmates; he was to be best man at the wedding. Frank asks what we wanted to drink, one for the road, says Frank; putting the drinks on the table Frank remembers he had a message for Tommy from another mate Jimmy McGowan. All I know its very important and you have to meet him as you clock on tomorrow Frank is delighted with himself for remembering.

Walking to work with Frank the next morning, Tom quizzed Frank trying to figure out what was so important; he had Jimmy's wedding invitation tucked away in his inside pocket. He was to meet Tommy in the canteen at lunch hour, which meant two as the welt was working very successful in box three. That night in bed once again I kept thinking about the old lady and I still couldn't believe that Tommy had not noticed her. I completed my prayers and sneaked another favour in asking Our Blessed Lady for a sunny day for the 19th of September 1964 at precisely one o'clock.

The following day at work, I was relating the events to my workmate Betty Ryan about our lovely day of shopping, and the kind gesture by Mr Hue in presenting us with a bottle of wine to celebrate our wedding. I was working over time it was just after seven when I arrived home, as I entered the kitchen I could hear Tommy's voice, 'don't take your coat off girl, we've got a meet with Jimmy at his at seven thirty, he's got a proposition to put to us', said Tommy rubbing his hands together. We arrived at Jimmy and Celia's house; it was a smart terraced house, consisting of two up and two down with an extension on the back. The kitchen had been added on complete with a double window dressed with white nylon cross over nets, a double sink unit with an electric heater directly over the sink. The back yard was immaculately whitewashed the concrete floor bleached white. At the bottom of the yard stood an outside loo, it was equipped with an electric light, the walls were painted cream, the floor tiled in red, and I could just picture Tommy and me living together in this neat little compact house.

Jimmy and Celia had spent months renovating the house; it had been their little palace.

'Right let's get down to business. The house is yours that is if you want it' said Jimmy, I started to bawl uncontrollably. Jimmy explained that Celia his wife had recently been suffering from really bad asthma attacks, and felt they had to move from the city if she was ever to improve and eventually recover. 'Get the wedding over and done with enjoy it because it will be the best days of your lives' says Jimmy he too was being a little emotional. We will make all the necessary arrangements later, I was bawling again. Jimmy and Tommy shook hands on the deal; the house in Kearsley Street was going to be ours.

Celia and Jimmy had solved our housing problem; they were so generous to us both. We have never forgotten their kindness, two very special friends.

The following Saturday, I visited St Peter's Church hoping to see the old lady and thank her and inform her about our good news. There was an entirely different lady pottering around, arranging flowers on the altar. Approaching her I enquired was the other lady around she looked at me in strange sort of way. I described the old lady, oh yes that sounds like Mrs Caterhan I was delighted, will she be in today I asked. The prim and proper sort of lady dried her hands on her pinny, looking me straight in the eye stating I doubt it sweetheart Mrs Caterhan passed away over twenty odd years ago. Turning away she continued on with her chores.

Dismissing me really I was quite taken back by her brusqueness after I recovered, I sat down and quietly thanked the lady who I knew I had spoken to that day I still honestly believe that Mrs Caterhan had a hand in our securing our home in Kearsley Street.

Over twenty-five years ago we decided to move and a deal was almost finalized when out of the blue both Tommy and I lost our jobs. Both of our children Tommy and Lisa were delighted, as they never wanted to leave our happy little home at Kearsley Street. Again for the second time we decided the time was right to move on, once again the move did not materialize I honestly think even now that Mrs Caterhan is still keeping an eye on us. We have lived here for over 43yrs, only a few weeks ago enjoying a drink in a pub in the City centre we got around to discussing the unknown and how things we can't explain happen. Tommy was in the chair and began the tale about the lady in Saint Peter's, Eddie and Joe both who were in our company looked at one another, both said together its always been haunted, they too had a tale to tell. When they were young lads living in the parish of St Peter's they served as altar boys. It was over the Easter period when the Crucifix was exposed at the foot of the altar. The congregation slowly joined the queue in order to kiss the wounded, nailed bleeding feet of Jesus. When the last person returned to the bench the priest signalled to both of the altar boys to return to their bench on the altar, but as they looked up another person was walking slowly down the aisle towards them on seeing him they remained on either side of the crucifix.

Wiping the feet of Jesus in preparation for him, they both recalled the incident clearly agreeing he was attired in a monk's type habit with his hood up and his face down, they couldn't see his face. By this time the priest was now furious by the actions of his two altar servers. As only they could see him it must have looked strange the two boys going through the motions as only they were aware of the stranger kissing the feet of the figure on the cross. After the service the priest informed them both to never to pull a stroke like that again in making him look the fool before a packed congregation. The two lads resigned in the vestry there and then because rightly so the priest thought they were fooling around, they never ever forgot the incident. The Church of Saint Peter's was thankfully saved from destruction, as a listed building, it was protected. It is now part of the regeneration in that area and recently having been refurbished. The beauty of the building thankfully remains untouched. The magnificent leaded windows remain, candles continue to flicker and burn still. The church is now a restaurant it will be interesting once again to visit Saint Peter's again after all those years I wonder if I will bump into Mrs Caterhan. How strange would that be?

A letter arrived from America, informing me about the kind deeds of this lovely lady, who had lived facing the church of St Peters taking care of the church by day and night. Mrs Caterhan was a very pious person and devoted most of her life to the church of Saint Peter's in Seel Street.

This impressive church of Saint Peters is now the popular restaurant the Alma De Cuba. The interior has lost none of its magnificent beauty.

At present it is now one of the most popular restaurants in the city the Alma De Cuba which caters for many celebrities, including the footballers. Liverpool Football Club celebrated their famous cup victory against West Ham there. It truly remains a fabulous setting the original altar still intact, the ambiance truly serene candles flickering through out the restaurant. It gladdens my heart to still have this beautiful church steeped in glorious history in our European City of Culture, yet again to be admired and rightly so by the thousands of visitors. I'm sure especially the sheer beauty of Saint Peter's, now named The Alma De Cuba, will intrigue them.

For what we are about to eat let us truly be thankful for!

CHAPTER FOURTEEN

THOSE WERE THE DAYS

After my first book had been on sale for a few months, it was quite rewarding to be recognized especially in town and congratulated. Even more satisfying when they add I'm not from Holy Cross, but every thing you wrote I could identify with. Inevitably the conversation usually ends with that immortal line. *'Those were the days'*.

I was browsing through the clearance rails in the T K Maxx store as always on the look out for a bargain. I was contemplating purchasing a 'chic little black number' hanging on the reduced rail. As I looked up I noticed a lady waving to me from the bottom end of the store. Her arms were laden with an assortment of clothes. I'm looking for an outfit for our Lauren's wedding, relating to me how the kids of today don't commit readily to the marriage institution.

I just loved your book I read it on holiday, cried my bloody eyes out! Honest to God, It brought back so many happy memories back for me she sighed. I was still pondering who this lady was, it was quite obvious she knew me well, inquiring how my husband Tommy was how, we had all frequented the same watering holes when we were 'young and foolish' in the early sixties.

Still holding conversation in the centre of the now busy store, it seemed somewhat rude of me to admit, and ask for a clue, I still had not recalled who this person was. I was just about to ask that old classic 'what parish were you from originally.' When she recognized another lady entering the store, shouting to attract her attention she immediately recognized her, more than I did. Hi Maureen, how's Mick keeping these days' she asked. There were two clues for me to work on.

I now knew both of their names, but still none the wiser. In the next breath Maureen said 'Don't you miss the old neighbourhoods, continuing on she mentioned how brokenhearted she was when her parish church of St Bridget's was wantonly destroyed to make way for the new ring road. Maureen ranting on that it was a sin against the almighty if ever there was one committed.

There was another piece to the puzzle. Maureen and I were now in full throttle about the rights and wrongs of the present generation agreeing that times have certainly changed from ours. Maureen reminds me how she was practically brought up by her Nin, hence still clinging on to the good old days. In the days of post war Liverpool. Looking back I realize how very naive we were, I'm not saying we were not inquisitive. If we asked a question and it was deemed a tad delicate, we were sharply reprimanded, 'little pigs have big ears' In other words do not comment on grown ups conversations. How we laughed, later Maureen left me with a classic tale, typical of our generation. How we were highly influenced by the clergy respecting their every word taken as gospel.

SAVED FROM THE FIRES OF HELL

Maureen recalls sitting around the table with both her parents and her grandparents, enjoying one of their favourite meals, bacon ribs, cabbage and fluffy mash potatoes. The conversation being about every day events, Nin inquiring had the dryers at the local washhouse been repaired yet, adding had Vera heard one of their close neighbours had been 'confined' yet? 'What does confined mean Nin asks Maureen, there was a clatter of cutlery hitting the plates at the same time.

An uncomfortable silence hung over the table, all eyes resting on the seven year old. Maureen's Nin by passed Maureen as if she was invisible at the table, Addressing Kathleen, Maureen's Mum, Nin in one of her condescending voices declared, 'You will have to watch your choice of words in future in front of this child; she's far too inquisitive for her own good'. Kathleen did not want to remind her mother that it was her choice of the forbidden 'confined' word in the first place.

Nin was ready to climb on her soapbox and bang on about times changing, adding and not for the better either. Kathleen instructs her daughter Maureen to help her clear the table. Maureen loved helping her Mam especially washing the dishes. Maureen standing on a sturdy stool that her Granddad had lovingly carved especially for her, helped wash the tea dishes.

Due to a team effort the dishes were soon stacked and stored away on to the kitchen shelf. Kathleen spoke quietly to Maureen explaining that the confinement word meant a brand new baby had been born and grown-ups used that particular word to describe the birth. Maureen had been nodding her head and was about to ask another question but decided against it when her Nin entered the kitchen.

I'll take Maureen to Benediction with me give you time to carry on and complete your ironing, says Nin, Thanks Mam that would be a great help answers Kathleen. Maureen loved attending Benediction especially if Father Tobin was celebrating; she loved the strong smell of the incense when he blessed you with it from the silver receptacle. Before the service Nin always gave Maureen coppers to light a candle to Our Lady of Lourdes. Benediction was always well attended; Maureen knew every hymn by heart word perfect, joining in with her Nin who she thought had a really lovely voice. Father Tobin was standing in the pulpit he seemed to have a 'bit of a cob on'. As he was thumping the pulpit with his fist so forcefully, in order to hammer his point home. Maureen moved closer to her Nin linking her arm through her Nin's. Still he continued on banging his fist making a really loud banging sound, Father did have a really serious cob on big time.

Nin whispered to her friend Molly who was sitting next to her, I wonder who spilt his milk this morning. Maureen thought it wasn't much of an excuse to carry on like that over a little spilt milk.

Usually Father Tobin was brilliant with everybody, having a laugh and a joke. Father was nearing the end of his sermon, but still somewhat serious, he pleaded with the congregation to knock on the door of the presbytery if they witnessed any signs of fornication in the parish.

Maureen decided that fornication might have been the word that was the real culprit for Father's bad mood and not the spilt milk. Maureen's obsessions with the meaning of words were once again to land her in serious trouble.

Father Tobin was once again his old self smiling wishing God's blessings to his parishioners and giving Maureen a special pat on the top of her head. Father Tobin was Maureen's favourite priest and was 'made up' once again to see him laughing with no sign of his previous bad mood. When they arrived home Kathleen had finished her ironing which was now neatly stored away in the airing cupboard. Kathleen volunteered to make every one a nice cuppa, her mother stifling a yawn, her Dad sitting in his favourite chair beside the fire. Reading the local evening paper 'The Echo', Maureen noticed her Granddad looked really jaded, (Maureen only learning that particular word last night) he worked so hard at the Liverpool docks, she overheard her Nin mention to her mum the hard work was taking its toll on Granddad, what ever that word meant. Maureen too felt tired too tired in fact to inquire exactly what toll meant. Maureen added toll to her list of words after fornication to be explained at a later date. After drinking her warm and welcomed milky cuppa, which was accompanied by a gorgeous thick piece of golden toast.

Maureen kissed both her grandparents, Granddad reminding her to eat all the crusts up, as it would help make her hair curly. Nin reminded her as she did every night to recite an eternal rest for the forgotten holy souls. The following day Granddad arrived home early for his tea, the ship he had been working on had a quick turn around he was delighted to be home so early parked in front of the fire eagerly checking his betting slips. Ann, Maureen's friend called by to ask if she would like to accompany her to the chippy, Granddad instructed them to cross on the zebra crossing. Scottie was a busy road to cross especially at teatime.

Inevitably there was always a massive queue at Jim's Palace chippy because of the quality of his fish and chips. Whiling away the time in the queue Maureen began relating to Ann about her nearly setting fire to the cuff of her new coat while lighting a candle. Ann instantly took a fit of the giggles at the thought of Maureen being set on fire. Father Tobin carried on shocking on the pulpit last night; Maureen relates Father's antics, including the word fornication and how the word made him really mad. Doesn't sound like our Father Tobin does it Mo, he's always dead nice, said Ann as they both moved slowly along the still massive long queue in Jim's Palace.

When Maureen arrived home her Mam had already set the table for tea, her Dad had just arrived home, removing his dirty working boots onto last nights newspaper.

Kathleen passed Joe a cuppa, 'oh that's a lovely cuppa girl tastes like nectar sliding down my throat', says Joe. Nin looking over her glasses at him and asks' You haven't been spooning my bees honey in to your cup on the sly have you, it's the only luxury I allow myself. Stop tantalizing her Joe laughs Kathleen, but Nin wasn't joking she was deadly serious. Maureen sat down next to her Dad, Kathleen declares well isn't this unusual for us all to be sitting at the table together, instead of dribs and drabs like most nights. Joe and Granddad were discussing what ships were in the port.

The meal was delicious, everybody was in a lovely amiable mood thought Kathleen, Maureen sitting up nice and straight for once and not having to be reminded. Maureen pipes up to no one in particular, Father Tobin was in a shocking mood last night at benediction, Maureen had their full attention, Granddad said he must have got out the wrong side of the bed. "No it wasn't that at all, Granddad"

Maureen in like a shot couldn't resist and I think it was something to do with the word fornication Granddad.

Granddad, what exactly does fornication really mean? There was a deathly lull in the conversation; Granddads face was now looking quite ashen.

Jesus, Mary and Saint Joseph what is this child's obsession with wanting to know the meaning of every conceivable word in the English Dictionary mumbles Granddad.

Don't be cursing Mick in front of the child, says an embarrassed Nin.

Our Maureen has just inherited an inquisitive mind Pop and I think it's a really a good sign that's she is going to excel at English. Joe rests his case and quickly escapes to the back kitchen for a well deserved cig. Kathleen brought out the stool a nightly ritual, placing it directly in front of the sink. Kathleen reprimanded Maureen for disrupting the meal. What have I warned you turning teatime into an English lesson, Maureen love; you know full well how it upsets your gran,

Kathleen was furious with Maureen for spoiling the good mood at the table. Maureen concentrates on clearing the debris from the plates before steeping them in the hot sudsy water.

Are they really vexed with me now Mam asked Maureen in quite a sheepish voice.' Yes they are answers Kathleen under her breath trying hard to suppress her laughter while stacking the dishes away into the cupboard. Maureen was still perched on the stool, Kathleen was busy scrubbing the draining board, Nin was always and ever going on about how important it was that the sink and draining board be left spotless after washing up. The wood was bleached white through the daily procedure.

Maureen watched her Mam's every move, when Kathleen looked up Maureen seized the moment while there was only the two of then in the kitchen. Mam what does the word fornication really mean, is it something naughty? Kathleen explained it's not the nicest of words it means- Kathleen thought how can I explain to a seven year old about fornication. Well it means when you see the courting couples together having a goodnight kiss and a cuddle in the entry behind the flats. Clearing her voice to carry on, she quickly explains, after the second house pictures ends at the Gem. Well suppose that's the best possible way I can explain it. Maureen sat digesting what her Mam had cautiously explained.

Climbing down from the stool Maureen asked permission to call for her friend Ann. As it was the 'lighty nights' the kids were allowed to play out a lot longer, especially in the summer holidays (teachers rest mothers persecution) Maureen explained the offending word in the way Kathleen had related to her.

Ann agreed with her best friend that every single one of the courting couples were in grave danger of burning in the fires of hell; because of the real bad sin they were committing. The thought of all the girls and lads who lived in their flats being in grave danger frightened the life out of Maureen.

DIVINE INTERVENTION

Ann and Maureen fearing for the welfare of their friends and their close cousins felt it was their duty to report them to Father Tobin who had the power to save them all from the burning inferno of hell. Together the girls linking arms presented themselves at the priest's house. Ringing the bell they waited, they were on an important mission. It took a while for the door to be finally opened by the housekeeper. She had been engrossed listening in to her favourite quiz show on the wireless; at the sight of the children she was really infuriated. What do you want? She asked in a narky voice, Maureen being the spokeswoman answered I want to see Father Tobin Its extremely important. Is it now said the vexed housekeeper, Fathers far too busy, so clear off. At that very moment Father Tobin, appeared. What can I do for two of my favourite little people said Father inviting them both in. The housekeeper hurrying away in a huff hoping she had not missed the most exciting part of the quiz. Maureen sat back on the chair making herself comfortable, while Ann remained standing admiring the gorgeous holy pictures on the walls. Maureen began, I've come to tell you that I know where there's plenty of bad *fornication* taking place. Father Tobin almost fell off his chair.

How do you know of this Maureen?

I haven't seen it for myself Father. Father Tobin let out a tremendous sigh of relief. My cousin Tony and Ann's cousin Joan, well, there's two whispered Maureen. Teresa and Joe, and a few more, there not all of our relations, but they are very good mates and we're frightened for them. Almost in tears Maureen whispers, honest to God I don't want our Tony to end up in hell.

Maureen was on a roll now giving the correct details and the precise location; the exact time the fornication took place was when the Gem picture house lets out, not the first one but the late performance. Maureen wasn't quite sure of the exact time the last house ended.

WHO LET THE DOGS OUT?

Father Tobin owned two beautiful Kerry Blue pedigree dogs. Assuring both girls especially Maureen for being concerned about her cousin Tony's welfare, he himself would attend personally to the grave matter immediately and by God he did. Adding God would in deed reward Maureen for worrying about her cousin's spiritual welfare. Maureen and Ann returned home well pleased with their good deed for the night. The following morning there was quite a commotion in the flats. Alice one of the neighbours was holding court on the landing her stout arms folded on her ample chest; Maggie was being brought bang up to date on the mayhem that had occurred the night before at the back of the flats.

Kathleen and her Mam joined the two women to hear exactly what had happened. Alice was in her element she had a prime position watching from behind her lace curtains. Why didn't you knock for me, I love a good scrap? Alice swore on her Jack's life that she hadn't been nosing.

Father Tobin showing off one of his treasured Kerry Blue dogs.

No you wouldn't, not in your nature Alice, replied Katie in a sarcastic voice. There was murder going on here I could not believe my eyes when I saw Father Tobin in attendance with his two dogs, they were barking, the girls were screaming, the lads legging it, scampering pronto when Father Tobin was ordering them all to remain were they were and the dogs would not attack them. Alice was in her element revealing all of the gory details of the previous night events.

Mollie declared Father Tobin was in his rights to clear the lads and girls, oh for Gods holy sake said Alice have you never been young yourself. When all the details were fully revealed, Father Tobin had collared Kate's grandson Tony and Joan, Maggie's granddaughter. The neighbours were mortified that their off springs were made an exhibition of by the parish priest, oh the shame of it all, my God we will be the talk of the parish at Sunday mass.

After the commotion of last nights escapades had eventually died down, Kate and Alice over a cuppa talked fondly about their precious grandkids, Kate mentioning that her Tony was giving his Nin a wide berth until she had calmed down.

Kate could never fall out with her grandson, she adored him, in fact she worshipped the ground he walked on. Alice was quite pleased that her lovely granddaughter was walking out with Tony; grudgingly she had to admit that he was quite a good-looking lad. Tony had good prospects too he was in his last few months of his apprenticeship at Tyson's the local building firm. There was a knock on the door Kate and Alice had drained the teapot. Kathleen popped her head around the door announcing it was Maggie and she was crying her eyes out.

Ushering Maggie in, she sat quickly into the chair visibly shaken.

Our poor Teresa's new coat well it's ripped to pieces by Father Tobin's dogs, and Molly's Gerard, his suit is in shreds, brand new only on his back once sniffed Maggie. He'd saved for weeks working overtime for weeks on end, God love him, he bought it from Roberts and Bromilys. Teresa's coat was brand spanking new too, God love her too she has only paid one payment to the clubman moaned Maggie drinking a fresh cup of tea. Alice put a comforting arm around her distressed friend stating, no one has died and if were honest it has been a bit quite around here lately. The women were still puzzled questioning how on earth did Father Tobin manage to find out about 'Lovers Alley', the lads and girls had stood there for decades without any interference from friend or foe.

The women sat consoling one another, in agreement, they're only young once and convincing themselves that the kids were doing no harm really were they?

Maureen was listening, hovering behind the door hearing how the lads and girls clothes were ruined but they had managed to escape without as much as a scratch on them. Maureen had convinced herself that Father Tobin's dogs were holy dogs and therefore they would not have harmed them, Maureen was glad none of her friends or her cousin had sustained any serious injuries. In fact Maureen was quite pleased with the out come the, ruined clothes were not much of a sacrifice to make in order to escape the wrath of hell. The saving of her cousin, and her close friends souls was now assured no burning inferno for them, they were off the hook. Her mission had been well and truly accomplished.

On the downside Nin was dreading the coming Sunday mass probably knowing the family would be the talk of the parish. Who cares if you look at the bigger picture, you will realize that the lads and girls of Saint Bridget's had been rescued in the nick of time from the jaws of the Kerry Blues. It took a joint effort by herself and her mate Ann and of course the man himself Father Tobin. The rescue mission was to remain their secret forever (until now). I apologise about letting the cat out of the bag (or I should say Kerry Blue dogs) after all these years.

FATHER TOBIN

Father Tobin was a formidable figure not just in the parish of Saint Bridget's but also around the neighbouring parishes. Father Tobin was loved and highly respected in the parish of Saint Joseph's were he served as Parish priest for over a decade. Father Tobin was always in the forefront of many battles when our city was once divided in fierce and bigoted religious stand offs. Father Tobin knew no bounds especially in the political arena; in fact he shone when it came to lobbying for equal rights for Irish Catholics. He was a fearless man big in stature as well as heart.

Saint Bridget's was the venue to be seen at on a Saint Patrick's night. After an enjoyable ceilidh some of the local lads being the worse for wear after one or two bevies, leading inevitably to a free for all outside the church hall. Rolling on the floor the lads literally knocking ten bells out of one another, until 'The Big Feller'appeared on the scene. Stepping deftly in to the centre of the melee, first things first removing his clerical collar, he waded in grabbing the worst offender, separating the trouble makers, a few good left hooks thrown expertly by the big man and the barny ends amicably the worst offenders sheepishly begging Father Tobin to forgive and forget, truth be known he quite enjoyed the melee, sorting the men from the boys.

I'm sure there are reams of untold tales involving the highly respected and much loved parish priest of Saint Bridget's, he was indeed quite a character.

I'd like to share an amusing story involving another character of the district Jimmy Donnelly, my father in law [who I never had the pleasure of meeting]. Jimmy was a hard working docker, supporting his wife Mary Alice and their eight children. Times were hard back then the workforce never guaranteed a full weeks work. Jimmy was quite a resourceful chap never missing an opportunity to pick up a few extra goodies especially for his precious brood. One such opportunity occurred when a pack of six quality fine Irish linen shirts accidentally fell in to Jimmy's lap, heaven sent his prayers answered.

Arriving home, he closely inspected the booty. His find, the fine handmade shirts must have been tailored for a bloody giant for Gods sake, they were a size eighteen collar, who the dickens would they fit?

Mary Alice was busy in the kitchen only half listening to her husbands ranting over the linen shirts. Sitting at the table enjoying his fish [as it was Friday] Mary Alice suggested he visit Father Tobin, as later on he was paying a visit to one of his favourite watering holes.

The Maid of Erin, known locally as Hogan's, a family run establishment (Tom Hogan emigrated to Australia I still regularly correspond with Tom posting him the 'Scottie Press' each month). Jimmy rubbed his hands with glee, in anticipation of a 'nice few extra quid'

Father Tobin opened the front door of the presbytery, 'How are you Jimmy on this grand night?', inquired Father. 'I'm fine and thanks for asking' says Jimmy, 'I've a pack of quality Irish linen shirts and I immediately thought of you Father', said Jimmy quite cautiously.

'Well now Jimmy isn't that grand of you to give me first refusal', says Father Tobin covering his mouth with his hand at the same time inquiring, 'now these items haven't fell off a moving wagon, so to speak have they Jimmy'.

God forbid, Jimmy answered a trifle too quickly. A quid each to you Father, but to any one else the asking price would have to be in the region of two guineas. Father Tobin laughed heartily accepting the shirts delighted with the done deal.

Later in the evening Jimmy joined his Mam and older brothers, Robert and Michael at their local pub in the parlour, Jimmy immediately rang the bell to summon the barmaid, drinks all round, that was the order of the night the extra bevies were Jimmy's treat. Jimmy called to Paddy to join them in a drink of his favourite tipple. Paddy was delighted and not too fussed to ask why Jimmy appeared to be quite 'flush' this very evening.

The aftermath of the true tale is quite funny. The following night Father

Tobin entered the pub, almost removing the sturdy door from its frame. Forget the hinges. Inquiring of Jimmy Donnelly's where abouts, in quite thunderous tones.

Paddy as nervous as a kitten of the priest's irate mood, he soon cleared the bar when he shouted to the punters; you should be home with your wives and family. Paddy placed a small measure of Irish whisky directly in front of the incensed cleric, answering quietly that he had not clapped eyes on the bold Jimmy as yet.

Paddy after a little cajoling persuaded Father Tobin to take a pew and to enlighten him to what misdemeanour Jimmy Donnelly had committed, to upset him so. Father Tobin loosened his collar, not always a good sign thought Paddy.

Informing Paddy that the exquisite linen shirts which he grudgingly admitted were of the highest quality, that Jimmy had recently sold him, were flaming *shrouds* Paddy desperately tried to suppress his laughter, not unnoticed by Father Tobin, who was now calling Jimmy Donnelly fit to burn. Threatening if he comes across him he surely will be wearing one of the perishing shrouds. As his fiery temper slowly abated he began to roar with laughter for Father Tobin really did have a great sense of humour and began to see the funny side of the shirts or in this case shrouds.

The elusive Jimmy had managed to keep his head down for weeks on hearing through the grapevine that the 'Big Feller' was indeed on his case. Jimmy finally bit the bullet and somewhat reluctantly called into the presbytery. You hard faced rascal roared Father Tobin, If I'd have got my hands on you last week Jimmy, I'd have wiped the deck with yer as God is my judge! Lucky for you, you scoundrel Jimmy Donnelly I've managed to cut my losses and sell the goods on to our eminent neighbourhood funeral director.

Father Tobin and Jimmy were buddies once again. The story later became legendary; especially at wakes! Jimmy Donnelly became *the talk of the parish*.

Local kids of the parish.
Notice the old gas lamp at the top of the 'Bush'.

Father Tobin and his assistant
priests taken outside the presbytery.

Lily McCann and her retinue; St Bridget's
procession.

Saint Bridget's Church preparing
for their annual procession

CHAPTER FIFTEEN

WEDDING CAKE

The impressive gravestone where generations have visited for many decades legendary tales kept alive from one generation to the other only and ever referred to as Wedding Cake grave, how sad that that the monument is recognised yet the persons name is never mentioned.

Isn't there always a tragic story that somehow captures your heart, such stories are the one's which have been handed down from one generation to the other. Times of sadness, especially at wakes, when folklore is high on the agenda in terms of sadness and the more macabre stories come into their own.

Sad stories especially love stories that don't end in the happy ever after mode. They are the ones that strangely everyone wants to hear about, even though they have heard the tale time and time again. The more tragic and bizarre the tale is the much better it is as this adds more to the ambience of the occasion

Wedding Cake's story is truly the one that I think would fall into the tragic scenarios.

I can vividly recall my Mam taking me to Ford cemetery, along with her best mate Annie Moran. Sunday afternoon just after lunch we took the tram to Ford cemetery.

The journey seemed to take forever; Ford cemetery located on the outskirts of the City of Liverpool. How morbid you may think to spend an afternoon walking around a graveyard for a five year old, far from it, no I loved it especially when I spotted the ice-cream van parked at the entrance.

First off we visited the more elaborate graves; some of these graves were absolute works of art. Most of the graves were sculptured in marble having been shipped in from Italy in the late 1800s. The more decorous ones were more likened to shrines, some standing over eight feet high. My Mam and Annie were familiar with every one of these monuments belonging to the more affluent members of the different neighbouring parishes.

One such grave was very unusual. I can only ever remember it being referred to as [God love her] Wedding Cake's grave. The unfortunate young woman who had legendarily died so tragically, at the age of twenty-eight. The grave was quite a unique one even for the1920s, which her parents had erected in her loving memory, and surely must have cost a fortune. There was no presence of anything religious statue wise.

To the side of the grave is a statue of a girl draped over a wedding cake.

This unfortunate woman who was legendarily jilted at the altar by her young man. Again in the folklore of the parishes, she supposedly died of a broken heart; in fact she did pass away on the most romantic day of the year the 14th of February St Valentine's Day. How sad this forlorn girl looks draped over a concrete wedding cake, had now become a legend throughout the inner-city communities.

Her grave almost becoming a shrine to the throngs of visitor's to the cemetery. Yet she was only ever to be known as 'Wedding Cake' her name never uttered.

Both my parents along with my brother John are interned at Ford cemetery, after each visit, I still to this present day pay my respects at this unknown girl's grave and recite an Eternal Rest for her.

I was visiting our family grave and replacing the flowers with fresh ones.

My daughter Lisa picked up the flowers announcing she was going to place them on Wedding Cake's grave. I was totally flabbergasted by this statement, as I had never mentioned about the tragic story to Lisa.

She quietly informed me that her Nan had for years (since she was three years of age, even younger than me), Had taken her to visit the grave and was aware of the sad saga of Wedding Cake's demise.

Unknown to me my daughter Lisa had been visiting the grave since she too had been a little girl. Like many before her she too had become intrigued by the story behind the girl whose fate was to this present day still talked about, as if it had only recently occurred. Her name never being uttered only referred to as (poor Wedding Cake, God Love her).

During the Christmas period of 2006 my daughter was once again visiting the cemetery to pay her respects at her godson Sean's grave.

Afterwards she paid a visit to Wedding Cake's grave were she laid a Christmas poinsettia plant. Lisa recalls staying for a while to say a prayer and mull over this young woman whom she now felt strangely so close to.

Wondering really what was the true events surrounding this young girl's premature death and was the circumstances of her death really a broken heart?

Through being jilted at the altar, this was the tragic story that has been associated to 'Wedding Cake' (Lillian) since her death. After reciting her prayers Lisa wished her a Happy Christmas praying that at least she had found happiness in heaven. Asking her for help to guide her life and help her make the right decisions in the near future.

I still couldn't believe what my daughter was relaying to me. After all these years Wedding Cake had almost become her posthumous mate!

A strange event occurred just before the Easter 2007 holiday.

When once again armed with flowers she made her customary visits to her late family. Leaving Wedding Cake to the last, after placing the flowers at the grave and reciting a few prayers for her friend's soul (as she now had began to look upon her as a departed friend) her mobile phone rang causing her to jump. The ringtone sounded louder in the tranquil quietness of the deserted cemetery.

The call received was from Linda, Lisa's cousin, Linda was inquiring if she was calling in for a cuppa on her way home, Lisa explains that she almost put the fear of God into her by calling her when she was standing right in front of Wedding Cake's grave.

Linda asked Lisa to take a photo of the grave. Requesting she take one at an angle to enable her to recognize what section it was sited so she too could visit the grave. Lisa set her mobile phone camera focusing on the centre of the grave, moving on to the bottom to reveal the statue. On taking the last photo Lisa whispered I'd love to know what you looked like Lil, I imagine you were so lovely;

I really feel I know you. Rest In Peace Lily, see you next time.

After a quick spurt in order to catch the bus, Lisa gratefully sat on the seat clearly out of breath. Promising herself a new pair of trainee's to resume training in sprinting around Stanley Park, with her Dad as that run had clearly highlighted she was way out of condition.

Put the kettle on shouts Lisa through the letterbox of Linda's house, after a nice hot cuppa and a tasty bacon buttie she had now got her breath back.

Lisa and Linda were deep in conversation about Lisa's pending visit to New York City. Sophie our young niece had taken Lisa's phone scanning through the earlier taken photos. She too had heard the sad story of the girl everyone refered to as Wedding Cake, and wanted to know every tiny detail much to the annoyance of her two Aunties' who were not taking the remotest notice of Sophie. Still scanning the pictures, Sophie asked why they put the photograph in the centre of the headstone. Still really not listening to Sophie, Lisa asked what she was on about; Sophie asked the same question, referring to the photograph.

No replied Lisa, they did not place photos on the graves in the olden days.

There is a black and white photo here says Sophie holding up the phone.

At last she had their attention good style now! Lisa and Linda together shot off the settee grabbing the phone from Sophie's hand.

There before their very eyes in the centre of the screen was an old-fashioned type portrait of a girl with a 1920s styled fringe and bob type hairstyle popular of that particular era. My God Lisa said to the now awestruck Linda, I can't believe it Linda, honestly I asked her (Wedding Cake) what she looked like, can you believe it, is this really Lillian Carey the girl they refer to as Wedding Cake. Everyone who looked at the photo immediately could clearly see the portrait styled photo, the face and shoulder pose of the late twenties era.

The lettering very clear that read Elizabeth (Lillian) Carey beloved daughter of Marcella and John Carey died 14th of Feb 1928.

Lillian Carey who had died at the young age of 28 yrs, allegedly from a broken heart, after being jilted at the altar. Again the jilted part of local folklore passed on down throughout the decades from one generation to the other.

This was the same version as told to me by my Mam. I'm delighted that there is now a lovely face (for the bigger picture as they say) Surmising that this picture is Lillian, a girl known locally through out the north end of the city as Wedding Cake.

Once again after all these years Lillian Carey has yet again become the talk of the parishes!

After recent revelations about the picture appearing on Lisa's phone (which in seconds was transferred to hundreds of peoples mobiles in Liverpool). Again the sad love story of Lillian was mulled over in offices and factories all over the city, once again (Wedding Cake's demise) was set to intrigue yet another generation.

Lillian's grave has never since been seen without a flower. Maybe another generation too has been captured and intrigued by Wedding Cakes story, I think so do you?

The memorial stone erected to their daughter by her parents in her memory was indeed very melodramatic, but maybe her parents deliberately chose to forever make an impact of her plight. A statute of a distraught girl draped over a concrete wedding cake. If this truly was their intention, then indeed they were successful, in leaving behind a lasting memorial to their loving daughter.

As neigh on eighty years after the sad passing of Lillian, the legend and indeed the mystery surrounding the story of Wedding Cake still to this present day continues to intrigue yet another generation…

OH BY THE WAY

I sincerely hope you have enjoyed this nostalgic walk through the decades as much as I have in writing about them. So many parishes in our communities especially in the inner-city are sadly no more. These are the places were so many of our personal memories began in our own parish churches. Receiving the holy sacraments through different stages of our lives when the time arrives all to swiftly for us to take our final journey, returning back to our roots to complete the pattern of life.

The last stitch in place (metaphorically speaking) back to were we once proudly belonged.

I hope by looking at the most precious collection of photographs which different people have kindly entrusted to me in order to have their own parishes included. Just by looking at these sensational sepia photos you can not help but be overcome by them, witnessing the drab tenement flats totally transformed by gaily coloured flags, flowers and buntings.

The artificial flowers so exquisite and lovingly created you can almost smell the perfume.

The fun that went into the making of the decorations was brilliant, sitting in the doorways of the flats under strict supervision by our Mams and close neighbours

We were taught the art of flower and buntings arrangements. So many laughs when our first attempts looked more like cauliflowers than roses. We all played our parts from the youngest to the oldest members of the parish. Maybe that was the key to our local communities being so close knit.

Each parish who were celebrating a special occasion was also our joy too, to share in the celebrations travelling to witness the awesome sights and compare it to our own parish decorations however afterwards 'declaring theirs not a patch on ours'. Oh yes believe me there was fierce competition between neighbouring parishes when it came to parish decorations and May processions. My dear Mam was truly the 'boss' in artificial flower creating, her flowers was displayed in many of the surrounding parishes.

I loved accompanying my Mam and her mates with their broods to inspect the lavish decorations visiting the different parishes, especially at night.

It was something special to witness beautiful altars surrounded in fairy lights twinkling in and out, coloured votive lamps burning in their red and blue glass holders.

Of course there was 'JARS OUT' celebrating in the streets dancing and singing accompanied by various musical instruments which added even more to the euphoria of the joyous occasion.

There was plenty of friendly banter when one of the parishioners spotted one of her 'washie' mates declaring not for the first time, not a patch on Holy Cross's decorations we'll put them up next time! All good fun between the parishes, never admitting maybe out of earshot they would admit grudgingly though; a tiny bit of praise for their fabulous efforts they were gorgeous.

The opening of a new church or a priests jubilee a parish centenary (any excuse really) to unfold the flags and hang the buntings once again from the washing lines.

Our Irish ancestors left us a precious heritage in their traditions which enabled following generations to carry on the dynasty of lavish outdoor ceremonies which our parish of Holy Cross was famous for. It was the actual taking part which was a bonus, walking in the processions accompanied by the various bands; especially the Irish pipes and drums made your heart swell with pride. (Faith of our fathers)

Sadly our sacred traditions have slowly ebbed away especially the spectacular out door May and June processions the pomp and majestic ceremony.

Thank God for the memories.

The parish churches of years gone by were the vibrant heartbeat of the communities, social clubs footie teams run by the clergy, including snooker and darts teams, indeed those were the days my friends! Before the invasion of telly and now computers plus the hi-tec games, the kids these days don't have to budge off the settee they just push a button on the remote control and they play footie, box, or play tennis that's what they call progress I suppose.

Excuse me while I polish my rose coloured spectacles for the last time after an enchanting time in being catapulted way back into time through the most fabulous collection of photographs of magical times in being lulled by the soft reminiscences of gentler times in and around the local parishes of our illustrious city of Liverpool.

Gildart Gardens in all its glory. Buntings galore what a sight?